CONTENTS

Library of Congress Cataloging-in-Publication Data

Names: O'Hara, Vincent P., 1951- author.
Title: Battleship Tirpitz / Vincent P O'Hara.
Other titles: Naval history magazine.
Description: Naval history special edition. | [Annapolis] : [Naval Institute Press] [2022]
Identifiers: LCCN 2022007842 | ISBN 9781591148708 (paperback)
Subjects: LCSH: Tirpitz (Battleship) | World War, 1939-1945—Naval operations, German.
Classification: LCC D772.T5 O43 2022 | DDC 940.54/5943—dc23/eng/20220328
LC record available at https://lccn.loc.gov/2022007842

INTRODUCTION

This is a *Naval History* Special Edition about the German battleship *Tirpitz*. It has been nearly 30 years since the last battleship sailed in an operation of war and 75 years since the destruction of *Tirpitz*. Time and hindsight have caused many to question the utility of battleships. Popular opinion holds that aircraft carriers rendered them obsolete. Some have wondered why Germany wasted steel on battleships and did not fill its slipways with submarines. In fact, a navy is a long-term investment, especially one built during a time of peace in anticipation of a future war. Capital ships, submarines, aircraft, escorts—all are different types of assets. Capital ships are the most expensive and take the longest to develop; during World War II no navy, not even the U.S. Navy, completed a battleship

laid down after the war had started. Like any good investment portfolio, diversity is key. Had Germany built nothing but submarines, for example, the navy could not have protected the nation's vital maritime traffic; it could not have projected power overseas, as in the invasion of Norway; it would have threatened British traffic in only one dimension, and one-dimensional threats are the easiest to counter.

The story of *Tirpitz* is testimony to the power of battleships. She was a ship that never fired her guns at an enemy vessel yet exerted a power that required a fleet to offset. She influenced Allied deployments and resources in a way that no other enemy vessel did. The story of how she was able to do this starts with the story of battleships as a weapon system.

CHRONOLOGY

- **14 June 1936:** Contract placed.

- **2 November 1936:** Laid down at Kriegsmarinewerft (navy shipyard), Wilhelmshaven.

- **1 April 1939:** Launched, christened by *Großadmiral* Tirpitz' daughter.

1941

- **25 February:** Commissioned, *Kapitän zur See* Karl Topp commanding.

- **20 March:** Trials in the Baltic begin.

- **23–26 September:** Flagship of the "Baltic Fleet" under the command of *Vizeadmiral* Otto Ciliax.

1942

- **14 January:** Operation *Polarnacht*. Leaves Wilhelmshaven for Trondheim escorted by four destroyers.

- **30/31 January:** First bombing attack. Sixteen RAF heavy bombers fail to locate the battleship.

- **6 March:** *Tirpitz* sorties with three destroyers to intercept the Allied convoys QP8 and PQ12.

An early view of *Tirpitz*. Her balanced profile is very apparent here. (Peter Schenk Collection)

- 9 March: Albacore torpedo bombers from *Victorious* unsuccessfully attack *Tirpitz*.

- 13 March: Arrives at Trondheim.

- 30/31 March: Unsuccessfully attacked by 33 Halifax bombers.

- 27/28 April: Unsuccessfully attacked by 29 Halifax and 11 Lancaster bombers.

- 28/29 April: Unsuccessfully attacked by 23 Halifax and 11 Lancaster bombers.

- 2 July: Operation *Rösselsprung*. At 1800, *Tirpitz* departs Trondheim under the command of *Vizeadmiral* Otto Schniewind with *Admiral Hipper*, four destroyers, and two torpedo boats.

- 5 July: *Tirpitz, Scheer, Hipper,* nine destroyers, and two torpedo boats depart Altafjord. The Soviet submarine *K-21* unsuccessfully attacks *Tirpitz*.

- 8 July: Anchors in Bogen Bay near Narvik.

- 23 October: Operation *Globus I. Tirpitz, Scheer*, and six destroyers sail to Trondheim.

1943

- 24 February: *Kapitän* Hans Meyer assumes command of *Tirpitz*.

- 11/12 March: Departs Trondheim for Narvik.

- 23 March: Operation *Silesia*. Task force transferred to Altafjord.

- 6 September: Operation *Sizilien. Tirpitz, Scharnhorst*, and nine destroyers under the command of *Vizeadmiral* Oscar Kummetz sail to attack Allied installations on Spitzbergen.

- 22 September: *Tirpitz* attacked and heavily damaged by British midget submarines.

- November 1943–February 1944: Under repair in Altafjord.

1944

- 12 February: Unsuccessfully attacked by Soviet bombers.

- 15 March: Trials in Altafjord begin.

- 3 April: Attacked by 40 bombers from British carriers and hit ten times.

- 1 July: Repairs completed and trials begin.

- 22 August: Unsuccessfully attacked by 32 Barracudas from British carriers.

- 24 August: Attacked by 33 Barracudas from British carriers and hit twice.

- 29 August: Unsuccessfully attacked by 26 Barracudas from British carriers.

- 15 September: Attacked by 27 Lancasters from Yagodnik, near Archangel. Hit by Tallboy bomb and severely damaged.

- 15 October: After temporary repairs, *Tirpitz* departs Altafjord and sails to Tromsø, anchors off Håkøy as a floating battery.

- 29 October: Unsuccessfully attacked by 32 Lancasters.

- 12 November: Attacked by 32 Lancasters. Hit and sunk by two Tallboy bombs.

GERMANY'S CAPITAL SHIPS AND THE "WASHINGTON-TYPE" BATTLESHIP

The German 32,000-ton superdreadnought *Baden*. She was the last German battleship constructed during World War I. Her main battery was eight 38-cm guns, like that of *Tirpitz*, but of an earlier type. (NHHC)

In 1939 the battleship was the queen of the seas. Battleships were designed to project power. They were the biggest and most powerful ships afloat. Throughout most of their 70-year span of maritime dominance, they constituted the measurement by which the world judged naval strength. In 1914 at the beginning of World War I, Germany had the world's second-largest battleship fleet and some of the best designs in the type afloat. Germany lost that war, and one of the objectives of the victors, particularly Great Britain, was to ensure that no fleet of modern and powerful German battleships would ever again ply the world's waters. To that end the Treaty of Versailles restricted Germany to a squadron of six overage predreadnoughts to defend its Baltic coasts. In fact, the victors had little stomach for an arms race of any kind. It was too expensive, and, in the minds of some, World War I had broken out in the first place because of Germany and Great Britain's battleship-building race. This led to the Washington Treaty of 1922 which restricted the construction of new battleships (with a few specific exceptions). What followed became known as the "battleship holiday."

The Washington Treaty allowed the signatories to start replacing their oldest battleships in 1931 and specified that these replacements could displace no more than 35,000 tons standard and be armed with main batteries with at most 16-inch guns. Up through the end of World War I, navies had accepted a speed of only 22–23 knots for their battle lines. This meant that designers could focus on armor and armament rather than speed. However, the Germans and the British also built lightly armored but very fast battle-cruiser types that during World War I showed that speed mattered in naval combat. Battle cruisers remained a distinct type until the 1930s, when high-pressure steam and lightweight turbines made it possible to give a heavily armed and armored battleship a battle cruiser's speed. The upshot was that by the end of the battleship holiday, speed had joined armor and guns as the paramount design considerations of a modern battleship. The catch was that the machinery required to drive a 35,000-ton ship at 30 knots was much heavier and required more room than that needed for 23 knots. To stay within treaty displacement limits, guns and armor characteristics had to be compromised. The case of the British ships *Nelson* and *King George V* are good examples. *Nelson*, laid down in 1922, displaced 33,500 tons. *King George V* from 1937 displaced 36,500 tons. The two had similar armor protection, but *King George V* was five and a half knots faster but had only 14-inch weapons while *Nelson* had a 16-inch battery.

Italy laid down the first Washington battleship, *Littorio*, in 1934. This image, showing *Littorio* and her sister *Vittorio Veneto* engaged in firing practice in 1940, conveys the raw power of the battleship. (NHHC)

After 1934 all the major naval powers—first Italy, then France, Germany, the United Kingdom, and finally the United States began constructing "35,000-ton" battleships. (Japan began to construct secretly a much larger class of superbattleships, but that is beyond the scope of this discussion.) These new classes of modern battleships, the last generation to be built en masse, can be called "Washington-type" battleships—they were all, to one extent or the other, designed within the treaty's limits.

The rest of this section will consider the characteristics of these ships, glance at their operations, especially against each other, beginning with an assessment of where *Tirpitz*' design stood in relation to those of other nations.

Tirpitz fired a relatively light shell but had more armor, as a proportion of total displacement, than any of her peers and was relatively fast. It is difficult to say that one design was necessarily better than another, because they were all built with different goals in mind. For example, the range of the U.S. ships was outstanding, but they were designed with an eye to Pacific operations, whereas the *Littorios* were constructed to fight the French in the western Mediterranean and needed speed more than range. The Axis ships had good armor but were also considerably overweight. The design that packed the most, in terms of speed, armor, and gunnery strength, into the smallest package was the French *Richelieu*. As far as general toughness, reliability, and quality of workmanship and materials go, the American ships were superior. Electronics and radar are other factors these comparative tables do not address. The Americans had the most advanced radar by 1942. The Germans started strong but by 1942 had fallen behind the British, while the Italians and French lagged even farther. In general, the designs had more similarities than differences, an artifact of the treaty limitations. None of the designs were ideal—all were compromises.

The most famous encounter between Washington-type battleships occurred when the German *Bismarck* fought the British *Prince of Wales* and *Hood* on 24 May 1941. Another came three days later, when *King George V* and *Rodney* took on *Bismarck*. Finally, the *South Dakota*–class ship *Massachusetts* faced *Richelieu*'s incomplete sister, *Jean Bart*, in November 1942. Other than those actions, there were no direct encounters between Washington-type 35,000-ton battleships. In each case, however, a battleship was either sunk (*Hood*, *Bismarck*) or severely damaged (*Jean Bart*) by battleship gunnery.

The *Jean Bart* / *Massachusetts* affray was not much of a duel. *Jean Bart* was immobile and had only one operational turret. She fired seven rounds at *Massachusetts*. With aerial spotting, *Massachusetts* landed seven 16-inch shells on *Jean Bart* from ranges between 23,000 to 27,000 yards. She also se-

WASHINGTON TREATY 35,000-TON BATTLESHIP CLASSES: CHARACTERISTICS

CLASS	Weapons	lb/brdsde	lb/min	AA Hy/Lt
Noth Carolina	9x16/45, 20x5/38	24,300	56,850	20/48
South Dakota	9x16/45, 20x5/38	24,300	56,850	20/44
King George V	10x14/45, 16x5.25/50	15,900	36,720	16/32
Richelieu	8x15/45, 9x6/55	15,600	28,518	12/24
Littorio	9x15/50, 12x6/55	17,649	29,114	12/36
Tirpitz	8x15/47, 12x5.9/55	14,112	31,224	16/28

CLASS	Disp Std	Belt/Deck	Armor	Speed	Range	Fuel
North Carolina	37,484	12.5"	41.0%	28	15000@15k	6,959
South Dakota	37,970	12.25"/5.3"	40.0%	27	15000@15k	6,959
King George V	35,500	15"/6"	33.8%	28	15600@10k	3,770
Richelieu	35,000	13"/5.9"	39.0%	31	5500@18k	5,866
Littorio	40,724	13.8"/6.4"	37.2%	29	4290@13k	3,300
Tirpitz	42,900	12.6"/4.7"	43.9%	30	9280@16k	3,280

USS *Massachusetts*, pictured in July 1944, belonged to the *South Dakota*–class. (NHHC)

verely damaged the large destroyers *Le Malin* (which was in port) from 26,000 yards and *Milan* from 28,000 yards and sank the destroyer *Fougueux* from 12,000 yards. In total she expended 798 16-inch shells and shot very well—mostly without radar assistance—for a ship on her shakedown cruise.

In the Battle of the Denmark Strait, *Bismarck*, sister ship to *Tirpitz*, sank the British battle cruiser *Hood* and badly damaged the new 35,000-ton Washington-type battleship *Prince of Wales*, in both cases by effective gunnery. *King George V* and *Rodney* ran down and sank *Bismarck* three days later, but by that time the German ship had been torpedoed by British naval aircraft and could not maneuver, making the final action very one-sided. The British navy's big takeaways from its encounters with *Bismarck* were that the Germans could hit early, deal out tremendous punishment, and absorb it as well—much as they had in the Great War. The ghosts of Jutland still haunted the Admiralty councils, and so, rightly or wrongly, London concluded it could not face *Tirpitz* with just one *King George V*–class battleship.

The 35,000-ton battleships also participated in several other surface actions: four in the Mediterranean involving the Italian ships, one in the Atlantic, one in the Pacific, and one in the Arctic Ocean.

- 23–25 September 1940, Battle of Dakar. The French *Richelieu*, supported by powerful shore batteries, two cruisers, three large destroyers, a destroyer, three submarines, and six sloops faced a British force consisting of two pre-Washington battleships, an aircraft carrier, four cruisers, nine destroyers, and two sloops. The British were trying to seize the important West African port of Dakar. In a three-day action the French finally drove the British off. *Richelieu* expended 24 380-mm, 102 152-mm, and 501 100-mm shells. She was struck by a British 15-inch round. This hit amidships and devastated a mess deck. It bulged but did not penetrate the armored deck. There were no casualties. The ship also suffered self-inflicted damage to three guns. A shell exploded in No. 7 gun, shattering the barrel, and Nos. 5 and 8 lost their rifling, causing serious damage.

Richelieu at the Battle of Dakar in September 1940. She belonged to the second Washington-type class to be laid down. With the outbreak of war her construction was rushed, but she was not completely ready for action when France fell to Germany in June 1940. (NHHC)

- 27 November 1940, Battle of Cape Spartivento. The Italian *Vittorio Veneto* accompanied by the old battleship *Cesare* fired a few extreme-range salvos at British cruisers. This caused the British ships to withdraw toward their own capital ships. The Italians refused to follow, thus ending the action.

- 28 March 1941, Encounter off Gavdos. *Vittorio Veneto* with three cruisers and seven destroyers tried to trap a British force of four cruisers and four destroyers. The action was fought at long ranges. The intervention of carrier aircraft allowed the British to escape with only splinter damage.

- 17 December 1941, First Battle of Sirte. The Italian *Littorio*, leading a force that included the old battleships *Doria* and *Cesare*, two heavy cruisers, and ten destroyers, encountered a British force of four cruisers and 12 destroyers escorting a supply ship toward Malta. *Littorio* fired at extreme range for ten minutes, while the British cruisers maneuvered to protect the supply ship and the destroyers made smoke. The action ended with the fall of night.

- 22 March 1942, Second Battle of Sirte. *Littorio*, leading a force that included three cruisers and seven destroyers, intercepted a British convoy escorted by five cruisers and 18 destroyers. In a two-and-a-half-hour engagement fought in a gale, *Littorio* damaged one cruiser but withdrew with the fall of night after delaying the convoy.

- 15 November 1942, Second Naval Battle of Guadalcanal. The U.S. Washington-type battleships *Washington* and *South Dakota*, screened by four destroyers, intercepted a Japanese bombardment force of one old battleship (*Kirishima*), four cruisers, and ten destroyers at night. Hit repeatedly by 8-inch and at least one 14-inch high-explosive rounds, *South Dakota* was forced from the action with radar and communications failures, though no critical damage. *Washington* sank *Kirishima*, scoring as many as 20 16-inch hits from close range.

- 6 December 1943, Battle of North Cape. *Duke of York* with four cruisers and eight destroyers ran down the modern German battleship *Scharnhorst* (her escort of five destroyers had become separated) attempting to intercept a Murmansk convoy. The battleship, firing in the dark, hit *Scharnhorst* in a boiler room at nearly 20,000 yards with radar-controlled gunfire, allowing destroyers to finish off the German ship with torpedoes.

The 35,000-ton battleships sunk by enemy action included the two German vessels *Bismarck* and *Tirpitz*, the British *Prince of Wales*, and the Italian *Roma*. Aircraft were the agents in the loss of the British and Italian vessels, both of which were under way at the time of their loss. *Littorio* was hit by three torpedoes in Taranto on 11 November 1940. She came to rest on the bottom and may have sunk had she been so damaged at sea.

Scharnhorst at Altafjord, Norway, shortly before her final action against *Duke of York* in December 1943. Note that she is painted all black. (NHHC)

UNITED STATES NAVAL INSTITUTE

The British battleship *Prince of Wales*, newly completed. She was the only Allied Washington-type battleship to be lost at sea. (NHHC)

Roma was hit by two German FX-1400 aerial guided bombs. These were weapons of a new type, dropped from aircraft and then guided into their targets. Each bomb weighed 3,000 pounds and carried 710 pounds of explosive. The fatal blow was caused by one bomb that struck *Roma* midships just aft of No. 2 turret. It penetrated, exploded, and caused a massive fire that detonated the forward magazine. The following explosion blew No. 2 turret overboard and broke the ship in half, killing 1,252 men. *Italia* (ex-*Littorio*) was also hit forward by such a bomb; it struck the deck on the starboard side abreast the No. 1 turret and exploded alongside, wounding one man and causing minor flooding.

Prince of Wales fell victim to six torpedoes delivered over the course of six attacks by Japanese aircraft, as well as to one bomb hit and several near misses that caused additional flooding. The fatal blow was struck by a torpedo that buckled the port outer propeller shaft. Flooding caused electrical failures that caused in turn a cascading series of failures of pumps, communications, and most of the antiaircraft guns. In a separate action on 8 July 1940, *Richelieu*, hit by a British aerial torpedo suffered similar effects from a single hit on her starboard quarter that caused a breach in the hull 30 by 28 feet between the starboard shafts. The blast effects were magnified by the shallow water.. The starboard inner shaft was badly buckled, and progressive flooding occurred. The ship was brought into the port of Dakar, but a lack of infrastructure (and pumps) made the flooding difficult to control and thereafter repairs time-consuming: they took almost a year, much longer than they would have in a better-equipped port.

The table on page 10 summarizes all damage inflicted on Washington-type battleships by enemy action during World War II.

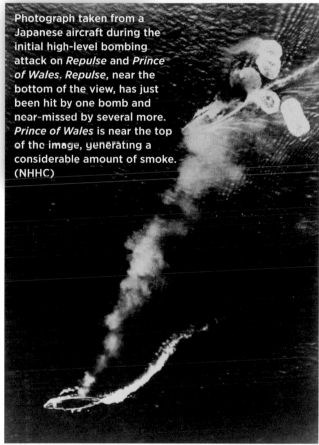

Photograph taken from a Japanese aircraft during the initial high-level bombing attack on *Repulse* and *Prince of Wales*. *Repulse*, near the bottom of the view, has just been hit by one bomb and near-missed by several more. *Prince of Wales* is near the top of the image, generating a considerable amount of smoke. (NHHC)

Incidents of damage inflicted, by agent (at sea/in port):

- 26 by aircraft (10/16)
- 9 by surface ships (7/2)
- 3 by submarines (2/1)

Ships were more vulnerable to aircraft in port.

Degree of damage inflicted by weapon (incidents/major damage/fatal damage):

- 9/3/1 gunfire (44 percent major or fatal)

DAMAGE INFLICTED ON WASHINGTON-TYPE BATTLESHIPS

Nation & Ship	Date	Where	By	Type	Type of Damage and Weeks to Repair				
					Flooding	Speed	Gunnery	Overall	Weeks
FR *Richelieu*	8-Jul-40	Port	BR	TT(A)	major	major	none	severe	10
FR *Richelieu*	25-Sep-40	Port	BR	shell	none	none	none	none	8
FR *Jean Bart*	8-Nov-42	Port	US	bombs	minor	n/a	none	none	-
FR *Jean Bart*	8-Nov-42	Port	US	shell	minor	n/a	moderate	major	-
FR *Jean Bart*	10-Nov-42	Port	US	bombs	major	n/a	major	major	n/R
GB *Prince of Wales*	24-May-41	Sea	GE	shell	moderate	minor	major	major	6
GB *Prince of Wales*	10-Dec-41	Sea	JA	TT(A)+B	total	total	total	sunk	n/a
GB *Duke of York*	26-Dec-43	Sea	GE	shell	none	none	none	slight	4
GE *Bismarck*	24-May-41	Sea	BR	shell	moderate	minor	none	minor	n/R
GE *Bismarck*	26-May-41	Sea	BR	TT(A)	moderate	moderate	minor	major	n/R
GE *Bismarck*	27-May-41	Sea	BR	shell	total	total	total	sunk	n/a
GE *Tirpitz*	23-Sep-43	Port	BR	mine	major	severe	severe	severe	20
GE *Tirpitz*	3-Apr-44	Port	BR	bombs	moderate	moderate	minor	moderate	12
GE *Tirpitz*	24-Aug-44	Port	BR	bombs	none	none	minor	slight	-
GE *Tirpitz*	29-Aug-44	Port	BR	bombs	none	none	minor	slight	-
GE *Tirpitz*	15-Sep-44	Port	BR	bombs	severe	major	moderate	major	n/R
GE *Tirpitz*	29-Oct-44	Port	BR	bombs	moderate	total	minor	minor	-
GE *Tirpitz*	12-Nov-44	Port	BR	bombs	total	total	total	sunk	n/a
IT *Littorio*	11-Nov-40	Port	BR	TT(A)	severe	major	none	sunk	18
IT *Vittorio Veneto*	28-Mar-41	Sea	BR	TT(A)	major	major	minor	major	15
IT *Littorio*	14-Apr-41	Port	BR	bombs	none	none	minor	slight	3
IT *Littorio*	18-Apr-41	Port	BR	bombs	none	none	none	slight	-
IT *Vittorio Veneto*	14-Dec-41	Sea	BR	TT(S)	moderate	moderate	none	moderate	13
IT *Littorio*	22-Mar-42	Sea	BR	shell	none	none	none	slight	1
IT *Littorio*	15-Jun-42	Sea	BR	bombs	none	none	none	slight	-
IT *Littorio*	16-Jun-42	Sea	BR	TT(A)	major	moderate	none	moderate	9
IT *Littorio*	5-Jun-43	Port	US	bombs	none	none	none	slight	-
IT *Vittorio Veneto*	5-Jun-43	Port	US	bombs	moderate	minor	none	moderate	4
IT *Roma*	5-Jun-43	Port	US	bombs	major	minor	none	major	10
IT *Roma*	23-Jun-43	Port	US	bombs	none	none	minor	slight	-
IT *Littorio (Italia)*	9-Sep-43	Sea	GE	bombs	moderate	minor	none	minor	n/R
IT *Roma*	9-Sep-43	Sea	GE	bombs	total	total	total	sunk	n/a
US *North Carolina*	15-Sep-42	Sea	JA	TT(S)	moderate	moderate	minor	moderate	6
US *South Dakota*	26-Oct-42	Sea	JA	bombs	none	none	none	slight	-
US *Massachusetts*	8-Nov-42	Sea	FR	shell	none	none	none	slight	1
US *South Dakota*	15-Nov-42	Sea	JA	shell	none	minor	major	moderate	4
US *South Dakota*	19-Jun-44	Sea	JA	bombs	none	none	none	slight	-
US *Indiana*	19-Jun-44	Sea	JA	A/C	none	minor	none	minor	-

n/R = never repaired; n/a = not applicable (ship sunk)

UNITED STATES NAVAL INSTITUTE

Damage done on USS *South Dakota* during the Second Battle of Guadalcanal, 15 November 1942. This hole was caused by an 8-inch shell. (NHHC)

- 9/5/2 torpedo/submarine mine (78 percent fatal or major)
- 20/4/2 bomb/kamikaze (30 percent fatal or major)

Overall, torpedoes were the most dangerous weapon to a Washington-type ship and bombs the least.

Incidents of damage inflicted on ships in port versus under way:

- 19/4/2 at sea (32 percent fatal or major)
- 19/7/2 in port (47 percent fatal or major)

Statistics such as these illustrate general trends. In the early and mid-1930s the designers of these battleships had a good idea of the threat imposed by naval gunfire and torpedoes. They did not envision heavy bombers carrying six-ton bombs or radio-controlled missiles, but in general the Washington-type battleships throughout World War II proved tough and generally able to meet the threats that confronted them. Moreover, the idea that their use, and the measure of their success has to do with how often and how effectively they used their main weapons is faulty. Battleships were expressions of power. They represented potential and intimidated with that potential. More than one important naval action was decided not by the power of a battleship's guns in action but by the refusal of one side or the other to face that power. It is by that standard that the success or failure of the type in general, and of *Tirpitz* especially, must be judged.

Tirpitz shortly after completion. (NHHC)

DESIGN AND CONSTRUCTION

*T*irpitz was the largest and the most modern battleship built by Germany, the last in a long line stretching back 50 years to the commissioning of *Kurfürst Friedrich Wilhelm* in 1894—the first of Germany's 51 oceangoing battleships and battle cruisers.

DESIGN

Germany decided to build a new class of battleship up to the 35,000-ton limits of the Washington Treaty in the spring of 1934; this was before Hitler's 16 March 1935 abrogation of the Treaty of Versailles. The initial requirements set forth by Admiral Erich Raeder, the German navy's Chief of Staff since 1928, were for a ship armed with eight 33-cm (13-inch), 12 15-cm, and 16 10.5-cm guns, heavy armor with a 350-mm belt, armored decks of 120 and 100-mm, and barbettes with 350-mm armor. Speeds had at least to match the new French battleships of the *Dunkerque*-class.

Kurfürst Friedrich Wilhelm, Germany's first oceangoing battleship. She was armed with six 11-inch guns and displaced 10,500 tons. She was given to the Ottoman Empire in 1910 and renamed *Heireddin Barbarossa.* A British submarine sank her in 1915. (NHHC)

Design work did not get far before it became clear that such heavy protection and high speed could not be shoehorned into a 35,000-ton vessel. For example, reducing the belt to 320 mm with 33-cm guns and a speed of 30 knots resulted in a ship that penciled in at 36,400 tons. The solution to this dilemma was to call the design "35,000" tons no matter what the displacement eventually ended up being.

By 1935 the navy had increased its main-battery requirement to 35 cm (13.7 inches), while accepting a speed of 28 knots. In March of that year 38-cm (15-inch) guns entered the discussion—an upgrade that would drive the displacement north of 42,000 tons. In April 1935 Raeder and his staff agreed to order a 41,000-ton ship armed with eight 35-cm guns. The armor would be 320 mm in the belt and on the barbettes, and armor on decks would top out at 120 mm. Of course, many aspects of the design, such as the layout of the secondary batteries and details about the armor and machinery, remained under discussion. Even this basic configuration did not last long, however, because by 8 May Raeder had approved 38-cm guns and a 20-mm reduction in the belt and barbette armor. The projected displacement of such a design was still over 41,000 tons.

The Germans continued to fiddle with the design's details up until the time the keel was laid. For example, in June 1936 the turboelectric drive was removed from consideration and a geared-turbine system adopted instead. The slight weight saving allowed the belt to go back to 320 mm. The first ship, "Battleship F"

(Bismarck) was laid down on 1 July 1936 and "Battleship G" (Tirpitz) followed on 20 October. Bismarck's designed displacement was 41,700 tons.

GUNNERY

As launched Tirpitz carried eight 38-cm/47 guns in four twin turrets; 12 15-cm/55 low-angle guns in six turrets; 16 10.5-cm/65 high-angle guns in eight twin mountings; 16 37-mm guns in eight twin mountings; and 12 20-mm single-mounted guns. Torpedo launchers were not originally fitted; Tirpitz received two quad 533-mm mountings in October 1941.

Germany's last superdreadnoughts of World War I had carried 38-cm weapons, but Tirpitz' 38-cm (14.96-inch) SKC/34 47-caliber guns were of a new design, with faster elevation and training rate and a heavier shell. The turret's revolving weight was 1,064 tons. The gun's basic characteristics were:

- Training-gear rate: 5.4°/second
- Elevation rate: 6°/second
- Maximum/minimum elevations: 30°/–5.5°
- Firing cycle: 26 seconds
- Designed barrel life: 250 rounds
- Shell weight (lb/kg): 1,764/800
- Muzzle velocity (fps/ms): 2,690/820
- Maximum range (yd/m): 38,880/35,550 (at 30°)
- Ammunition: 940–950 rounds

TIRPITZ, PROFILE AND DECK VIEW AS CONSTRUCTED

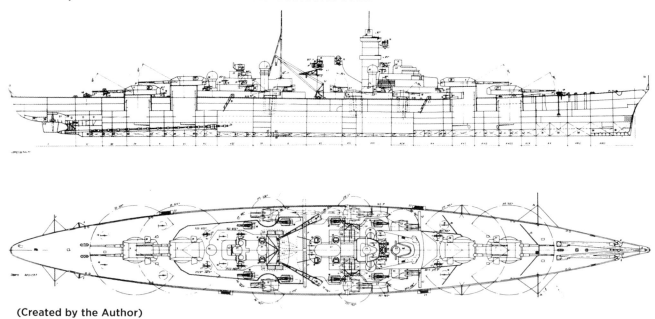

(Created by the Author)

The ship's secondary battery employed 15-cm SKC/28 55-caliber QF guns. The total turret weight was 105 tons. The basic characteristics were:

- Training-gear rate: 9°/second
- Elevation rate: 8°/second
- Maximum/minimum elevations: 35°/–10°
- Firing cycle: 7.5 seconds
- Designed barrel life: 1,100 rounds
- Shell weight (lb/kg): 99.87/45.3
- Muzzle velocity (fps/ms): 2,871/875
- Maximum range (yd/m): 24,060/22,000 (at 30°)
- Ammunition: 1,800 rounds, some APC but mostly HE nose- and base-fuzed and illuminating shells

The heavy antiaircraft armament consisted of guns of the 10.5-cm SKC/33 65-caliber type. The total mounting weight was 29.13 tons. This was the standard weapon on all larger German warships. Its basic characteristics were:

- Training speed: 8.5°/second
- Elevation rate: 12°/second
- Maximum elevation: 80 degrees
- Firing cycle: 3 seconds
- Shell weight (lb/kg): 33.3/15.1
- Muzzle velocity (fps/ms): 2,953/900
- Maximum range (yd/m) 19,360/17,700 at 48 degrees
- Ammunition: 6,270 shells with time fuze for aerial targets and 240 tracer rounds

The antiaircraft battery as designed was heavy for the time, but war experience exposed it as inadequate, and it was heavily supplemented as the war progressed. As designed and at launch the major close-range antiaircraft weapon was the 37-mm L/83 C30 gun. Its basic characteristics were:

- Shell weight (lb/kg): 1.636/0.742
- Muzzle velocity (fps/ms): 3,281/1,000
- Ceiling at (ft/m): 15,750/4,800 at 90 degrees
- Maximum range (yd/m): 7,100/6,500
- Rate of fire: 160/barrel/minute, 80 in practice.

The 20-mm L/65 Model C30 Oerlikon was a popular Swiss design used by the Americans, British, Italians, and Germans, among others. In German service its characteristics were:

- Shell weight (lb/kg): 0.2714/0.1231
- Muzzle velocity (fps/ms): 2,740/835
- Rate of fire: 280 rounds/minute
- Ceiling at (ft/m): 10,000/3,050
- Maximum range (yd/m): 4,800/4,390
- Ammunition: as designed, approximately 32,000 37-mm and 24,000 20-mm rounds

TORPEDOES

:In October 1941 *Tirpitz* was fitted with eight 533-mm torpedo tubes in two quad mounts (probably salvaged from destroyers lost at Narvik). She carried 16 reloads. The tubes were installed on the upper deck on each side amidships. They fired Type G-7 torpedoes, which had a speed of 44 knots at a range of 5,800 meters, 40 knots at 7,000 meters, and 30 knots at ranges up to 12,000 meters. The explosive charge was 280 kg of TNT. These weapons were meant for quickly finishing off merchant vessels damaged during oceanic commerce raids. However, the height of the launching point over the water would have compromised their effectiveness.

ARMOR

Total weight of armor on *Tirpitz* was 21,034 tons. This was distributed as follows:

- Belt: 320 to 145 mm (12.6 to 5.71 inches)
- Upper deck: 80 to 50 mm (3.15 to 1.97 inches)
- Armor deck: 120 to 80 mm (4.72 to 3.15 inches)
- Turrets: 320 to 130 mm (12.6 to 5.12 inches)
- Conning towers: 350 to 50 mm (13.78 to 1.97 inches)

Vertical protection was supplied by the main armored belt, which extended from frame 202.7 aft to frame 32. It tapered from a maximum thickness of 320 mm to 170 mm. An extension ran above the main belt between the upper and battery decks. Its thickness was 145 mm. The belt was 4.8 meters deep and extended 1.6 meters below the design waterline. It covered 70 percent of the

THE GUNS USED IN *TIRPITZ*

38-cm SK C/34

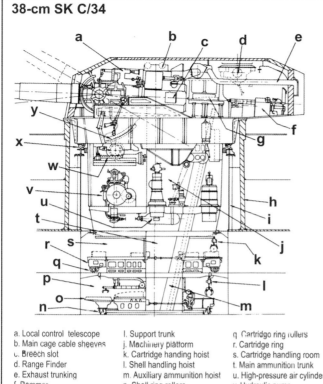

a. Local control telescope
b. Main cage cable sheeves
c. Breech slot
d. Range Finder
e. Exhaust trunking
f. Rammer
g. Shell in loading tray
h. Barbette
l. Support trunk
j. Machinery platform
k. Cartridge handing hoist
l. Shell handling hoist
m. Auxiliary ammunition hoist
n. Shell ring rollers
o. Shell ring
p. Shell handling room
q. Cartridge ring rollers
r. Cartridge ring
s. Cartridge handling room
t. Main ammunition trunk
u. High-pressure air cylinder
v. Hydraulic pump
w. Elevating gear
x. Turret bearings
y. Elevation arc

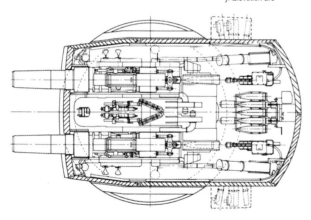

15-cm SK C/28

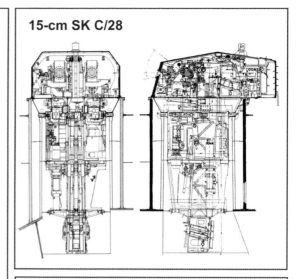

105-mm SK C/33 in C/37 twin mount

37mm SK C/30 Dopp. LC/30 mount

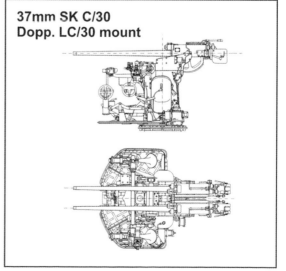

20-mm Flakvierling C/38

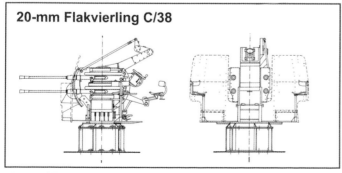

(Created by the Author)

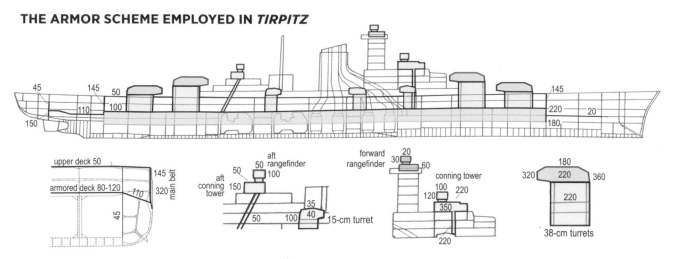

The goal was to protect as wide an area of the ship as possible, in contrast to the "all or nothing" schemes favored by the U.S. Navy, which focused on concentrating protection on the most vital areas, leaving the rest of the ship unprotected. (Created by the Author)

ship's waterline. Forward and aft of the main belt were thinner armored extensions. The aft belt extension was 80 mm from frame 10.5 to 32 and 2.1 m deep. It reached 1.5 m below the waterline. Forward, a 60-mm belt extended from the main belt. Forty-five-mm armor and port and starboard torpedo bulkheads inboard of the armored belt provided additional vertical protection. These armored bulkheads extended from the upper deck down to longitudinal IX. Total vertical protection was 8,969 tons.

Two armored decks supplied most of the horizontal protection. The upper armored deck was 50 mm thick for most of its length from frame 10.5 to 224. It weighed 2,478 tons. The other armored deck varied from 120 mm to 80 mm in thickness. It extended from frame 32 to 202.7. Aft a lower armored deck of 110 mm continued from frame 10.5 to frame 32. Total weight of the armored deck was 4,732 tons.

Armored bulkheads sealed the armored citadel at frames 32 (200 mm) and 202.7 (100/220/180 mm) Another armored bulkhead at frame 10.5 (45/150 mm) protected the steering gear.

The main-battery turrets were protected with armor ranging from 360 mm on the face, 220 mm on the sides, down to 130 mm on the roofs. The barbette shields were 220 mm. The 15-cm turrets were armored with face, side, and roof protection of 100, 40, and 35 mm, respectively. The aft range finder had sides of 100 mm and a roof of 50 mm. The aft conning tower had sides of 150 mm and a roof of 30 mm. The forward range finder had 200-mm sides and a 100-mm roof. The conning tower had 340-mm armor and was connected

to the command center by a trunk protected by 200 mm of armor.

MACHINERY

Tirpitz was capable of 30 knots at 163,000 shp. She achieved this speed using a geared-turbine system that drove three shafts. Her normal fuel capacity was 3,280 tons, but maximum fuel capacity was 7,780 tons. Her range was 9,280 nm at 16 knots, 8,525 nm at 19 knots, 6,640 nm at 24 knots, and 4,500 nm at 28 knots.

There were 12 Wagner-pattern boilers built by Deschimag, arranged by pairs in six boiler rooms. They operated at a pressure of 58 kg/cm^2 and a temperature of 450 degrees C and weighed 59.5 tons. The geared Brown-Boreri turbines occupied three compartments, the one driving the center shaft farthest aft and the two side turbines in compartments aft of the boiler rooms. There were eight diesel generators of 500 kW DC housed in electrical plants 1 and 2, which were to port and starboard of compartment VIII. Electrical plants 3 and 4 on either side of compartment XVI held five turbogenerators of 690 kW and one of 460 kW. Total output was 7,910 kW. The ship's light and power were direct current; some special equipment used alternating current.

RADAR AND SENSORS

When commissioned, *Tirpitz* was equipped with three FuMo 23 radar sets, one on the aft fire-control center and one at the foretop with the 10.5-m range finder, and one on the forward fire-control center with the

THE SHIP'S MACHINERY ARRANGEMENTS

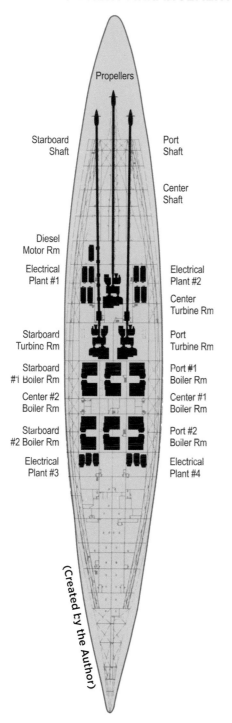

Propellers

Starboard Shaft

Port Shaft

Center Shaft

Diesel Motor Rm

Electrical Plant #1

Electrical Plant #2

Center Turbine Rm

Starboard Turbine Rm

Port Turbine Rm

Starboard #1 Boiler Rm

Port #1 Boiler Rm

Center #2 Boiler Rm

Center #1 Boiler Rm

Starboard #2 Boiler Rm

Port #2 Boiler Rm

Electrical Plant #3

Electrical Plant #4

(Created by the Author)

7-m range finder. The specifications of this device were:

- Range: 13 nm
- Accuracy: ± 70 m and ± 3°
- Wavelength: 81.5 cm
- Frequency: 368 MHz
- Output: 9 kW

She received a FuMo 27 in January 1942 above the 10.5-m range finder in the main gunnery control position and a FuMB 7 TIMOR.

- Range: 13 nm
- Accuracy: ± 70 m and ± 5°
- Wavelength: 81.5 cm
- Frequency: 368 MHz
- Output: 8 kW

In mid-1944 a FuMo 212/213 (Würzburg) was installed. The FuMo 27 and two of the FuMo 23s were replaced by a FuMB 4 (SAMOS), a FuMo 26, and a FuMo 30 at around the same time.

FIRE CONTROL

The fire-control system on *Tirpitz* consisted of three gunnery-control positions that fed information to two fire-control centers. These positions could direct both the main and secondary batteries. The main/secondary battery gunnery-control positions were in the conning tower forward, at the top of the foremast tower, and aft on the superstructure deck. The forward position had a 7-m stereoscopic range finder. The other two had 10.5-m units. The two forward positions had three ZG C/38G gunnery directors, and the aft position had two. The function of these positions was to obtain target information: range, bearing, inclination, and speed. Once firing had started, the directors would provide corrections to improve the accuracy. The positions fed this information to the fire-control centers. The major pieces of equipment in these centers were a pair of C38 ASR fire-control computers and a pair of C/38 Rw Hw Geber (RHG) bearing and elevation calculators. There was also a gyro room associated with each of the fire-control centers. The gyro rooms would supply corrections for the ship's pitch, yaw, and roll to the RHG calculators. These devices would then calculate stabilized bearing and elevation data and feed this to the ASR computers. The computers, in turn, would take information from the gunnery-control positions as well as direct input from operators for own course, own speed, wind speed, air pressure, and range rate. From all this the computer would calculate the necessary turret bearing and elevation and the appropriate moment for the guns to fire, on the basis of the target's predicted future position.

The C38 fire-control computer. The left dial is "own ship" and the right dial "enemy ship." The dial between them indicates firing range and bearing. The cranks at the bottom are, from left to right, used to enter range corrections, range rates, and bearing rates. (Norman Friedman/John Asmussen)

Origin of the Name *Tirpitz*

Großadmiral Alfred von Tirpitz. (NHHC)

Alfred Peter Friedrich von Tirpitz (19 March 1849–6 March 1930) was the architect of the first modern German navy. He started his career in the preunification Prussian navy in 1869 and was first a torpedo specialist. He was promoted to *Kapitän zur See* in 1888 and came to the notice of Kaiser Wilhelm as a strong advocate of a battleship fleet. He became Chief of Naval Staff in 1892 and was promoted to rear admiral in 1895. His innovations with respect to German naval policy were to make the construction of 19 battleships between 1898 and 1905 a matter of law and to secure popular support for such a policy. This set Germany on the course of conflict with Great Britain. A second bill, which legislated construction up to 1917, resulting in Germany's building the world's second-largest fleet. The justification for this massive and expensive expansion of the German navy was known as the "Risk Theory": that the German fleet would be powerful enough to harm irreparably any foe (i.e., Great Britain) and that this risk would dissuade said foe from going to war with Germany. Tirpitz became *Großadmiral* in 1911. His policies, however, while they did produce the world's second-most-powerful navy, encouraged Great Britain to embrace a lesser enemy, France, to oppose the greater enemy, Germany. Tirpitz fell from power in 1916, by when it was clear his policies had led to results opposite to those intended.

LAYOUT OF THE SHIP'S MAIN ARMAMENT AND FIRE-CONTROL ARRANGEMENTS

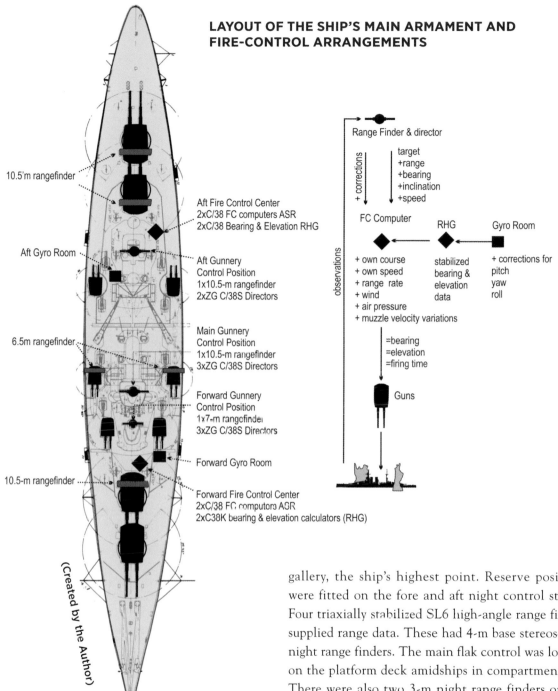

10.5'm rangefinder

Aft Fire Control Center
2xC/38 FC computers ASR
2xC/38 Bearing & Elevation RHG

Aft Gyro Room

Aft Gunnery
Control Position
1x10.5-m rangefinder
2xZG C/38S Directors

6.5m rangefinder

Main Gunnery
Control Position
1x10.5-m rangefinder
3xZG C/38S Directors

Forward Gunnery
Control Position
1x7-m rangefinder
3xZG C/38S Directors

Forward Gyro Room

10.5-m rangefinder

Forward Fire Control Center
2xC/38 FC computers ASR
2xC38K bearing & elevation calculators (RHG)

(Created by the Author)

Range Finder & director

+ corrections

observations

target
+range
+bearing
+inclination
+speed

FC Computer

RHG

Gyro Room

+ own course
+ own speed
+ range rate
+ wind
+ air pressure
+ muzzle velocity variations

stabilized
bearing &
elevation
data

+ corrections for
pitch
yaw
roll

=bearing
=elevation
=firing time

Guns

There were also 10.5-m range finders on turrets B, C, and D, and 6.5-m range finders on the port and starboard midship 15-cm turrets, but these were only backups to be used in case the guns needed to fire under local control. There was also a night fire-control center with specialized night-vision equipment and a computer to control the fire of star shell.

The 10.5-cm heavy antiaircraft battery had its own system, consisting of four ZAG (*Zeilanweisergeräte*) target information sights located on the foretop gallery, the ship's highest point. Reserve positions were fitted on the fore and aft night control stands. Four triaxially stabilized SL6 high-angle range finders supplied range data. These had 4-m base stereoscopic night range finders. The main flak control was located on the platform deck amidships in compartment XV. There were also two 3-m night range finders on the wings of the admiral's bridge and eight portable 1.25-m instruments used for the 37-mm guns. The 37- and 20-mm guns also had firing sights for the gunners.

TIRPITZ AS COMPLETED

- 823.5 ft/251 m overall length
- 792.7 ft/241.6 m waterline length
- 118.1 ft/36 m maximum beam
- 34.8 ft/10.6 m operational draft

- 29.5 ft/9 m designed draft
- 42,900 tons designed
- 52,600 tons operational
- Eight 38-cm (14.96-inch) SKC/34 47-caliber guns in four turrets
- Twelve 15-cm (5.9-inch) SKC/28 55-caliber QF guns in six turrets
- Sixteen 10.5-cm (4.13-inch) SKC/33 65-caliber guns in eight mountings
- Sixteen 37-mm L/83 C30 guns in eight mountings
- Twelve 20-mm L/65 Model C30 Oerlikons in 12 mountings
- Fuel oil: 3,280 tons as designed, 7,780 maximum
- Speed: 30 knots at 163,000 shp

- Endurance:
  - 4,500 nm at 28 knots
  - 6,640 nm at 24 knots
  - 8,525 nm at 19 knots
  - 9,280 nm at 16 knots

CREW

At full strength under wartime conditions the ship's company consisted of 108 officers and 2,500 other ranks. The ship's company was organized into ten divisions:

Divisions 1–4: Seaman branch, gunners, fire control, magazine and shell rooms, and senior officers

Divisions 5–7: Engine room and damage control personnel

A famous shot of *Tirpitz* taken from astern, 1940–41, showing the stern anchor in its recessed well, folding propeller guards, armor belt, and other details of hull and superstructure. (NHHC)

UNITED STATES NAVAL INSTITUTE

Division 8: Gun and torpedo mechanics, armorers, aircraft personnel

Division 9: Communications and radar personnel, coxswains

Division 10: Administrative and services including cooks, paymaster, tailors, barbers, stewards, masters at arms, boatswains, musicians, civilians, other specialists.

AIRCRAFT

Tirpitz was designed to carry four catapult-launched Arado Ar 196 seaplanes. The two-man crew of each in-cluded a Luftwaffe pilot and a naval officer as navigator/gunner. The Arado 196 had a top speed of 192 mph (167 knots). Its range was 580 nautical miles. It carried two wing-mounted 20-mm cannons and two 7.9-mm machine guns; given the right opposition (such as a British biwing torpedo bomber), it also functioned as a fighter. Its load was two 70-kg (154-lb) bombs. The hanger was 22 meters long and could hold all four aircraft.

HANDLING

Tirpitz was exceptionally stable, with a very slight roll even in heavy seas. She was responsive to the helm. With rudder hard over, heel was only three degrees and speed loss was 65 percent. However, she was difficult to control at low speeds or going astern.

COST

Tirpitz cost 191.6 million RM. To put this in perspective, *Bismarck* cost 196.8 million RM, the light cruiser *Nürnberg* 40 million RM, a type VII C submarine 4.7 million RM. In 1940, $2.5 RM = $1.00 U.S. USS *Massachusetts*, launched at roughly the same time as *Tirpitz*, cost $77,000,000. At the exchange rate quoted here, the price of *Tirpitz* was almost identical: $76,640,000 in 1940 currency.

Arado Ar 196 seaplane being catapulted from the deck of *Gneisenau*. (NHHC)

WORKING UP AND BALTIC SERVICE

APRIL 1940–JANUARY 1942

O n 1 April 1939, 80,000 spectators crowded the slipway at the Kriegsmarinewerft in Wilhelmshaven to see Hitler and a group of dignitar-
ies—current and retired admirals, Nazi Party functionaries, politicians,
and leaders of business and industry—celebrate the launching of the largest
warship ever built in a German yard. The daughter of *Großadmiral* von Tirpitz,
Mrs. Ilse Von Hassell, performed the christening. (She was the wife of diplomat

April 1939, launching of the hull of *Tirpitz*. (Aldo
Fraccaroli Collection, courtesy USMM)

Ulrich von Hassell, who was secretly a member of the German opposition to Hitler and would be executed in November 1944.) Because the ship was being launched into a basin that was less than twice as wide as the ship's beam, a 1/30 model of the ship and the basin had been constructed to predict the ship's behavior during and immediately after launch. Based on the results of the study, the hull was equipped with brake shields and floats, an anchor at bow and stern, and a swivel anchor. These precautions helped ensure a successful launch.

Tirpitz conducted machinery trials in the fitting-out basin as early as April 1940, a year after launch, but it was nearly two years before she was considered ready to begin sea trials, on 25 February 1941. The 22-month fitting-out process was a lengthy one. By comparison, *King George V* required 20 months,

Richelieu 18, and *North Carolina* 14. Only *Littorio*, at 36 months took longer.

All that time, well before she was ready for sea, *Tirpitz* drew enemy attention. Royal Air Force (RAF) harassment of the battleship commenced in October 1940, when three small bomber raids targeted the ship. One raid in November by five bombers was frustrated by what the pilots described as "impossible conditions." On 8/9 January 1941 seven Wellingtons attacked Wilhelmshaven and claimed hits or near misses on the ship—their assessment was overly optimistic. Eight Hampdens had even worse luck on the night of 16/17 January. Bad weather forced two to abort; one ditched in the North Sea with engine problems. Only two found the target, and they got no hits.

(top) Fitting out at Wilhelmshaven, 2 February 1940. (NHHC); (bottom) Fitting out continues; the superstructure is almost complete. (Aldo Fraccaroli Collection, courtesy USMM)

The British, keeping a watchful eye on *Tirpitz*, knew when the battleship's fitting-out was almost complete. This caused the tempo of RAF attacks against the ship to accelerate. On 29/30 January, 25 Wellingtons bombed the Wilhelmshaven area but missed the battleship. On 9 February, 13 aircraft took off to attack but did not score any hits. On 27/28 February, 30 Wellingtons from four different squadrons sortied to attack *Tirpitz*. Twenty-six actually found the target, but visibility was poor and there were "no reliable observations of results." The next night 23 bombers made the trip across the North Sea but could not locate the target because of low clouds and ground haze. Four aircraft dropped bombs in the ship's general vicinity. Between October 1940 and 1 March 1941 the RAF launched ten night raids targeting *Tirpitz* but failed to score a hit.

On 25 February 1941 *Tirpitz* was formally commissioned. *Kapitän zur See* Karl Topp, a veteran of World War I, was the ship's first captain. He had served in staff positions before receiving this highly desirable assignment. On 9 March 1941 he took *Tirpitz* from Wilhelmshaven to Gotenhafen via the Kiel Canal. The Baltic was safe, and on 20 March *Tirpitz* began to work up, starting with speed trials. These were followed by

(top) Detail of ship's superstructure; looking forward, the deck is cluttered. (Peter Schenk Collection); (bottom) *Tirpitz* in the final stages of fitting out. (Peter Schenk Collection)

Kapitän zur See Karl Topp getting acquainted with his crew, 25 February 1941. (Public Domain)

antiaircraft exercises using towed drones, damage-control rehearsals, repeated practice launches and recoveries of the ship's Arado seaplane, and shooting exercises with the target ship *Hessen.* For several weeks *Tirpitz* rehearsed an Atlantic mission, staying at sea and receiving supplies from tankers and merchantmen.

On 5 May Hitler visited the ship at Gotenhafen. The real reason for his trip to the former Polish port was to inspect *Bismarck* before her Atlantic raiding mission. The Führer toured *Bismarck* in the morning and discussed the upcoming raiding cruise with *Vizeadmiral* Günther Lütjens, who would be flying his flag in *Bismarck*. That afternoon Hitler reembarked on the yacht *Hela* to inspect *Tirpitz*, where he was received once again by Lütjens. Reportedly, Topp cornered Hitler in his cabin and begged that *Tirpitz* be allowed to join *Bismarck* and *Prinz Eugen* on their cruise. Hitler nodded but said nothing. Thirteen days later, Topp watched the two ships set sail for the North Atlantic; *Tirpitz* remained in the Baltic to continue her training.

Großadmiral Erich Raeder and Adolf Hitler touring the decks (*Signal Magazine*, Enrico Cernuschi)

Tirpitz under way for trials, circa March 1941. (NHHC)

Working up in the Baltic. *Tirpitz* alongside a friendly submarine. (USCG)

Tirpitz back in dry dock to fix defects revealed during the working-up process.
The ship would never again enter dock throughout her two and a half years of
service in Norway. (Peter Schenk Collection)

The North Atlantic operation was a failure. *Bismarck* and *Prinz Eugen* did not intercept a single merchant ship, much less a convoy. Although *Bismarck* sank the British battle cruiser *Hood*, she was herself hunted down and destroyed after a dramatic chase for which the British deployed three battleships, two battle cruisers, two aircraft carriers, three heavy cruisers, and many destroyers.

Despite the painful loss, the German navy did accomplish something important in the *Bismarck* episode: it established a viable threat that haunted British naval planners for the next three years. For example, in late August 1941 Admiral Dudley Pound, the First Sea Lord, and Winston Churchill had an exchange about *Tirpitz* after Pound advised the prime minister to retain three *King George* V–class battleships in the Home Fleet, two to take on *Tirpitz* and one in reserve: "If the *Tirpitz* did manage to break out she could paralyse our North Atlantic trade to such an extent that it would be essential to bring her to action at the earliest possible moment, and we could not afford to have one of the *King George V*'s absent from the scene of operations." In reply Churchill complained that his nation's newest battleships could not take on Germany's newest ship one on one, but noted that in any case there was no reason for the Germans to risk the ship at sea. "How foolish they would be to send her out, when by staying where she is she contains the three strongest and newest battleships we have, and rules the Baltic as well." They were speaking of a ship that was still working up.

In July, gunnery trials off Rugen Island revealed defeats that returned *Tirpitz* to Kiel, where she spent the rest of the month dry-docked at Deutsche Werke. The workup was further delayed, and she remained in Kiel until 17 September 1941. Even though *Tirpitz* was still not ready for combat by German standards, on that day the battleship departed on her first war mission, as flagship of the Baltic Fleet.

The Soviet Baltic Fleet

When Germany invaded the Soviet Union on 22 June 1941, the Soviet Baltic Fleet consisted of

- 2 old battleships
- 2 heavy cruisers
- 2 flotilla leaders
- 21 destroyers
- 7 guard ships
- 71 submarines
- 144 smaller warships (gunboats to motor torpedo boats, including mine warfare vessels)

The Soviets had five naval bases in the Baltic, three of them in the recently annexed Baltic States: at Libau in Latvia, Ust-Dvinsk in Latvia, and Tallinn in Estonia. There were also Hanko in Finland and the major base at Kronshtadt near Leningrad.

Tirpitz as flagship of the German Baltic Fleet, shown here leading *Admiral Scheer* and the light cruisers *Köln* and *Leipzig*. (Public Domain)

Upon the outbreak of war, the Soviets immediately started laying mines to block access to the Gulfs of Finland and Riga, and their first major losses happened that evening, when the cruiser *Maxim Gorky* and two destroyers ran into German mines. The cruiser was severely damaged and the destroyer *Gnevnyi* sunk.

Up through the end of September the major naval events were, first, the revelation of the ineffectiveness of the large Russian submarine force. Before winter stopped operations, the Soviet submarines sank one German submarine and three merchant ships (two of which ran into submarine-laid mines) at a cost of 27 boats lost. The Germans quickly came to disregard the enemy's undersea force and in July started letting merchant vessels sail unescorted. In July the Germans also initiated regular convoys into the Gulf of Riga and the seized port of Ust-Dvinsk. The Soviets opposed these convoys with destroyer patrols but failed to attack aggressively; the Germans maintained the traffic using only minesweepers as escorts. Finally, on 28 August, the continuing German advance forced the Soviets to evacuate Tallinn. The Germans contested this movement with mines and aircraft; the Russians lost at least five destroyers, ten smaller warships and 17 merchant vessels. More were damaged. On 13 September German troops landed on Moon Island and began the conquest of the Baltic Islands, a process that took a month. German aircraft attacked the main base at Kronshtadt and on 23 September sank the battleship *Marat*.

The pressure on the Russian fleet increased when the German command formed a Baltic fleet to oppose any Soviet attempt to sortie or seek asylum in Sweden (as might happen if Kronshtadt were in danger of being overrun). *Vizeadmiral* Otto Ciliax hoisted his flag on *Tirpitz* as commander of the new fleet. His force included the armored ship *Admiral Scheer*; the light cruisers

Soviet battleship *Oktyabrskaya Revolutsiya*. Had the Soviet fleet elected to sortie, she would have been the heaviest unit available to face the German ship. Fortunately for her crew, the Soviets stayed in port, where the ship did stellar service as a floating battery. (Boris Lemachko Collection)

Nürnberg and *Köln*; the destroyers *Z25*, *Z26*, and *Z27*; the torpedo boats *T2*, *T5*, *T7*, *T8*, and *T11*; and four motor torpedo boats. The light cruisers *Leipzig* and *Emden*, with four motor torpedo boats, formed a southern group available at Libau should need arise. By 23 September Ciliax had deployed his fleet off the Åland Islands, ready for a Soviet lunge.

Had the Russians challenged the Germans in the Gulf of Finland, they would have been seriously outgunned. The battleship *Oktyabrskaya Revolutsiya* and the cruiser *Kirov* were both damaged but could have sailed. They would have had an escort of 12 destroyers. Many smaller warships could have supported them, although it is unlikely they could have contributed to any fleet action. In the event, air raids on Kronshtadt on 23 September further damaged *Kirov*, *Oktyabrskaya Revolutsiya*, and one destroyer. On 26 September the German Baltic Fleet returned to Gotenhafen. There was no longer a role for large warships in the Baltic's submarine- and mine-infested waters.

After her excursion to the Åland Islands, *Tirpitz* returned to dock. In October her antiaircraft battery was increased and quadruple torpedo mounts were installed on each side of the upper deck amidships. She then went to Kiel and spent the month of November at Deutsche Werke Kiel (Dock C). On 21 December she resumed working up at Gotenhafen until on 10 January 1942 *Tirpitz* was finally declared fully operational. She transited the Kaiser Wilhelm (Kiel) Canal for the last time and arrived in Wilhelmshaven on the 14th.

German Naval Strategy at the End of 1941

Despite the loss of *Bismarck* in May 1941, *Großadmiral* Erich Raeder always intended to resume attacks against Allied shipping with the fleet's heavy units once they were operational. The battleships *Scharnhorst* and *Gneisenau* and the heavy cruiser *Prinz Eugen* were concentrated at Brest, and all would be fully repaired by the beginning of 1942. In his 17 September 1941 conference with Hitler he advised that Atlantic operations with battleships or cruisers would be possible then. Hitler asked whether it would not be better to station the battleships in Norway to defend the north, given that in Brest they were under constant peril from air attack. The meeting notes state that Raeder answered by pointing out that "the idea of using these ships to wage war against merchant shipping in the Atlantic is the correct one." In a 12 December 1941 report to the Führer, Raeder stated that the situation with regard to surface warfare in the Atlantic had been improved by Japan's entry into the war. He planned for the battleships at Brest, which would all be repaired by January, to work up and be ready to sortie into the Atlantic no later than March. *Tirpitz* would be assigned to Norway. One week later, when the two met in one of their periodic conferences, Hitler rejected his admiral's strategy of using battleships against commerce, because he expected that the British "if they go about things properly . . . will attack northern Norway at several points." He went on, "The German Fleet must therefore use all its forces for the defense of Norway. It would be expedient to transfer all battleships and pocket battleships there for this purpose." Moreover, if the Brest squadron could not return to German waters through the English Channel, "it would be best to decommission the ships and to use the guns and crews for reinforcements in Norway."

Raeder twisted and squirmed, but there was nothing he could do to change the Führer's mind, and so the return of the Brest squadron though the English Channel was scheduled. This effectively ended the grand admiral's strategy for the surface fleet.

This meeting also defined *Tirpitz'* strategic function:

- **To protect our position in the Norwegian and arctic areas by threatening the flank of enemy operations against the northern Norwegian area**

and by attacking White Sea convoys.

- **To tie down heavy enemy forces in the Atlantic so that they cannot operate in the Mediterranean, the Indian Ocean, or the Pacific.**

This strategic decision turned a significant portion of Germany's naval strength away from Great Britain's greatest point of vulnerability—its Atlantic communications with North America—to focus instead on a defensive role in a secondary theater.

Tirpitz to Brest: The Missed Opportunity
The Worldwide Balance of Battleships on 1 January 1942

The vision of a German flotilla of three battleships and two heavy cruisers based at Brest and poised to attack Great Britain's vital supply line to North America was one that terrified the British Admiralty. It was especially worrisome to the Allies in the context of early 1942, because the worldwide balance of capital ships had suddenly swung in favor of the Axis powers.

four were damaged, while the Japanese fleet was now on the German side of the ledger. Finally, *Scharnhorst* and *Gneisenau* had returned to service. It was a unique moment of opportunity for Germany, one that would never come again.

It is impossible to say what a German battleship foray from Brest in March 1942 might have accomplished. The

CAPITAL SHIP AVAILABILITY SEPTEMBER 1941 COMPARED TO JANUARY 1942

Axis Sep 41	Available	Operational	Axis Jan 42	Available	Operational
Battleships	5/5/na (10)	1/5/na (6)	Battleships	5/5/11 (21)	5/4/10 (19)
Carriers	0/0/na	0/0/na	Carriers	0/0/9	0/0/9
Allies Sep 41			Allies Jan 42		
Battleships	16/na	11/na	Battleships	12/11 (23)	8/8(16)
Carriers	9/na	5/na	Carriers	8/7	4/7 (11)

AXIS NUMBERS = GERMAN/ITALIAN/JAPANESE (TOTAL)   ALLIED NUMBERS = BRITISH/AMERICAN (TOTAL)

As shown by the table, the ratio of operational Allied capital ships (battleships and aircraft carriers) to those of the Axis in September 1941 was 16:6. In January it was 27:28. In November and December 1941 the British lost four capital ships (*Ark Royal* and *Barham* to German submarines and *Prince of Wales* and *Repulse* to Japanese aircraft) and two more (*Queen Elizabeth* and *Valiant*) put out of service for a long time by Italian frogmen). The Americans lost four at Pearl Harbor, where another

functioning of ULTRA might have led to a disaster: all the supply ships required to maintain the squadron in the mid-Atlantic might have been hunted down and sunk on the basis of signals intelligence, as happened in the middle of 1941. However, it is clear from the nearly suicidal British raid on St. Nazaire on 28 March 1942 to destroy the only dry dock in France able to accommodate *Tirpitz* that the British took the possibility of her coming out very seriously.

TIRPITZ TO NORWAY AND FIRST ACTIONS

JANUARY–MARCH 1942

The Channel Dash (Operation Cerberus) was a strategic withdrawal of Germany's heavy naval force from the Atlantic-coast port of Brest to Germany in February 1942. Photographed from the heavy cruiser *Prinz Eugen*, showing the battleship *Gneisenau* ahead and *Scharnhorst* in the distance. (NHHC)

On 14 January 1942 *Tirpitz* arrived in Wilhelmshaven ready to undertake her transit to Norway. Because naval staff had concluded that *Bismarck* had been spotted and revealed to the British during her transit of the Great Belt and Kattegat, *Tirpitz* began her first venture into the North Sea by the more secure route of the Kaiser Wilhelm Canal. She had to unload stores and ammunition at the canal's east end to reduce her draft just enough to make the passage and then reload them at the west end.

That night, in Operation *Polarnacht*, the battleship departed Wilhelmshaven bound for Trondheim escorted by the destroyers Z29, *Beitzen*, *Heinemann*, and *Jacobi*. The barometer was dropping, with a gale blowing its way east from the Atlantic to cover the British Isles. The only Allied submarine patrolling the approaches to Trondheim was the Dutch boat *O14*, but she was reinforced by *Trident* and *Seawolf*, and then by *Tigris* and the French boat *Minerve*. Nonetheless, *Tirpitz* arrived unsighted on 16 January. The British did not even know she had left Germany until the 17th or that she was in Norway until 22 January. This in itself caused a minor sensation. On 25 January Churchill wrote the Chiefs of Staff,

The destruction or even the crippling of this ship is the greatest event at sea at the present time. No other target is comparable to it. . . . The entire naval situation throughout the world would be altered, and the naval command in the Pacific would be regained. . . . The whole strategy of the war turns at this period on this ship which is holding four times the number of British Capital ships paralysed, to say nothing of the two new American battleships retained in the Atlantic. I regard the matter as of the highest urgency and importance.

The prime minister's call to action did indeed prompt action. The Chief of the Air Staff, Air Chief Marshal Charles Portal, met with Bomber Command. As Portal expressed it, "the following facts emerged": the only aircraft with sufficient range to hit *Tirpitz* in Trondheim were four-engine Halifax and Stirling heavy bombers. The only airfield close enough was Lossiemouth in northern Scotland at the mouth of Moray Firth—which, during the winter, was only periodically operational. A daylight raid was out of the question. However, the air chiefs were determined to launch an attack as the prime minister wanted on the first night

Trondheim, Norway, during the war. The Germans had big plans for Trondheim. It was to be their main Atlantic naval base, and they commenced a giant project to construct reinforced submarine bunkers. The surface fleet, however, mainly relied on geography for protection, basing ships in narrow fjords away from the city. (NHHC)

(inset) *Tirpitz* in Fættenfjord: The steep sides of the fjord allowed the battleship to berth right next to the cliffs, making her an extremely difficult target for aircraft. (*Signal Magazine*, Enrico Cernuschi) Two officers strolling the battleship's deck. The Germans also relied on camouflage to protect the ship. (NHHC)

with enough moonlight (weather permitting). This proved to be 30/31 January. Seven Stirling and nine Halifax heavy bombers made the 550-nm flight across the North Sea but, because of heavy clouds and severe icing, they failed to locate the battleship. One Halifax did not return.

Once she was in Trondheim, there was initially little *Tirpitz* could do, because the German naval staff had sent her destroyer escort to the English Channel for the forthcoming operation to bring *Scharnhorst*, *Gneisenau*, and *Prinz Eugen* through the channel from Brest back to Germany. In the event all three ships made it, although both battleships hit mines along the way. The Germans regarded this operation, known as the "Channel Dash," as a tactical success. Strategically, the operation was an admission of defeat by the government. There would never again be a heavy German surface force based at Brest to threaten Allied traffic in the Atlantic.

The Strategic Importance of Norway

Geography made Norway important to Germany. In World War I the British had boxed the German navy into the Heligoland Bight, where it never played the role in the war its size suggests it should have. With bases in Norway, such as Trondheim or Narvik to the north, Germany had much improved access to the Atlantic. Control of Norway's ice-free coastal waters also guaranteed year-round traffic in the high-grade Swedish iron ore that was vital to Germany's industry. Most of the year the ore could come safely through the Baltic, but in winter the Swedish ports that served the mines were iced in and the ore had to be transported to Narvik and thence to Germany along the Norwegian coast. Finally, in the context of 1942 and the war against Russia, Norway provided a base for operations against the northern front and for interdicting Allied convoys supplying the Soviet Union. A strong German presence in Norway also served to intimidate Sweden and ensure that nation's general compliance with German wishes. These reasons alone made it important to defend the long western flank of the Scandinavian Peninsula. However, in Hitler's eyes the paramount reason to base the navy in Norway was that Norway was the logical point for a British invasion. His beliefs were very much encouraged by a series of raids the British launched against Norwegian ports.

On 3 March 1941 in Operation Claymore, 3 and 4 Commando and 50 Norwegians raided the Lofoten Islands off the country's north coast. The commandos destroyed fish oil–processing facilities and some shipping against little resistance. Three hundred men from 12 Commando and some Norwegian personnel returned to the Lofoten

British forces approaching Vågo. (U.S. Naval Institute photo archive)

Islands on 26–28 December 1941 in Operation Anklet. They destroyed two radio transmitters, captured two small coasters, and sank a 145-ton armed trawler. More significant was a simultaneous operation (Archery) against Vågso and Måloy Islands in southern Norway by 3 Commando, elements of 2 Commando, and some Norwegian troops, 576 men in total. This operation faced a company-sized German garrison.

The commandos never eliminated the resistance and suffered 69 casualties; an additional 31 RAF personnel were killed and 11 aircraft were lost. The raiders destroyed two small patrol boats and five freighters (13,778 GRT).

These raids were pinpricks, but they confirmed Hitler in his conviction that Norway was a theater of destiny: hence his fierce insistence on the fleets being concentrated there.

Operation Archery

ADAPTED FROM REAR ADM. H. E. HORAN, U.S. NAVAL INSTITUTE *PROCEEDINGS*, APRIL 1961

Operation Archery, the British raid on Vågso Island, Norway, which took place on 27 December 1941, was the first operation undertaken by the Royal Navy, the Army, and the Royal Air Force working in co-operation during the course of World War II.

The selection of the target to be attacked was circumscribed because the only ships fitted to carry both landing craft and the requisite troops in the United Kingdom at the time were the small Belgian cross-channel steamers *Prinz Charles* and *Prinz Leopold*. As they were designed originally for the Dover–Ostend run, they had only limited endurance.

The nearest point of the Norwegian coast was the island of Vågso, which is situated due east of the port of Lerwick in the Shetland Islands. On studying all the available intelligence reports, it was found that the Germans were using this as a convoy assembly port for

their merchant ships which were making extensive use of the passage through the Inner Lead—the clear and calm route through the fjords and outer islands. It was in the town of Vågso that the German control staff was established; further, there were a number of fish factories established on the shores of Ulvesund—the channel between and the mainland. These factories were a source of both food and oil for the German population.

To protect the anchorage in Ulvesund from attack from the sea, the enemy had established a battery of four 4-inch, quick-firing guns on Måloy Island at the southern entrance to the Sound, and these were supported by two larger guns on the mainland, which commanded the entrance to the Inner Lead from the seaward. In addition, there was a small garrison in the town of Vågso itself. Organized opposition was therefore to be expected.

It was also well-known that the Germans had dispersed considerable air strength in Norway and that their nearest airfield was at Herdla, only about 40 minutes' flying-time from Vågso.

The objective, as given to the force commanders, was to sink, burn and destroy any enemy shipping found in the convoy assembly anchorage, and to put out of action the garrison (kill or capture) and the German installations in the port including the fish factories.

The plan finally decided on was to use a military force consisting of two Commando units—one to deal with the battery on Måloy Island and the other to deal with the German garrison in the town and the convoy control organization. The destroyers in the force were to enter Ulvesund and deal with any shipping they might find there. Supporting gunfire was to be given by the 6-inch-gun cruiser HMS *Kenya*, while air support was to be provided by shore-based aircraft of the Royal Air Force stationed in the north of Scotland and the Shetlands. These planes would be working at just about the limit of their effective range.

With all raiding operations, surprise and speed are of first-class importance. In this respect, the passage to Vågso had to be made in the dark and at high speed so that the landings could be made at first light. As the weather forecast was favorable for 27 December the force sailed from its anchorage after dark on 26 December.

Vågso burning. (U.S. Naval Institute photo archive)

The passage was uneventful; as the first streaks of dawn appeared on the eastern horizon, *Kenya* passed close to the submarine which had been stationed to act as a navigational aid, and the coast of Norway loomed up ahead.

The weather was ideal, with a calm sea, a clear atmosphere, and no wind—just the right conditions for a landing—while the snowcapped high land looked most attractive in the early morning light.

Punctually to the minute, at 0848, the bombardment by the ships began; it was just daylight in these high latitudes at this time of year. Under cover of twilight and the smoke bombs dropped in exactly the right places, the landing craft made their way ashore.

The bombardment lasted for just over nine minutes, and during that time, between 400 and 500 high-explosive shells landed on Måloy battery. When the landing craft were within 100 yards of the shore, the firing ceased and the troops landed to find the enemy dazed. It did not take long to put the guns out of action and collect the prisoners, and then the way was open for the destroyers to enter the Ulvesund. At about this time, the battery on the mainland at Rugsundo opened fire on our ships. The shore guns were quickly silenced by *Kenya*, but managed to get going again later in the day when they scored one hit on her.

On entering the fjord, between the island of Vågso and the mainland (Ulvesund), the destroyers found a German convoy approaching from the northward. All the ships in this convoy were either sunk or run aground, where they were quickly destroyed. In addition, other ships were found in the convoy anchorage off South Vågso, and these were quickly dealt with. Altogether, eight enemy ships—five merchant ships, two armed trawlers, and an armed tug—were disposed of for a total of 15,650 gross tons.

The offensive against shipping was not confined to the above ships. Certain Blenheim aircraft of Bomber Command, when flying patrols in conjunction with this operation, encountered and attacked another convoy of enemy ships making its way through the Inner Lead. Several of these ships were damaged, and at least one was sunk.

The Royal Air Force also gave very effective support to the operation by attacking the airfield at Herdla. Flying at very low altitudes of 250 feet, the aircraft dropped their bombs on the wooden runways and destroyed aircraft which were taking off. This attack undoubtedly reduced the scale of the air attack on our raiding ships, which also received direct protection from Beaufighters and Blenheim fighters of Coastal Command. During a series of fights which went on through the day, our aircraft shot down four HE-111s and prevented successful attacks on our ships lying off the beaches.

Besides the landing on Måloy Island, groups from the other Commando unit were landed just south of the town of South Vågso and fought their way through the town to their objectives. They were later reinforced by the troops which had dealt with the Måloy battery. The opposition put up by the enemy was pretty stiff, but in the end, all the objectives were reached and dealt with satisfactorily. These included oil-fuel tanks, ammunition stores, and a certain industrial plant owned by a quisling who was known to be operating for the Germans.

The quick withdrawal after any raid is about the trickiest part of the whole show; things become a bit disorganized during the fighting. By 1230, however, all enemy opposition had ceased. For over an hour, the landing craft had been employed evacuating the wounded, prisoners, and such civilians as wished to take an active part in the fighting against the Germans. It was now time to reembark. This was carried out very much according to plan despite interference from an enemy air attack. This air raid was broken up by the defending aircraft and the gunfire of the ships; neither damage nor casualties were suffered by the raiding forces. By 1445, all ships were on their way back to Scapa Flow under the escort of fighters of the Royal Air Force. There is nothing of note to record concerning the return voyage.

(top inset) *Tirpitz* camouflaged at her moorings in the Fættenfjord. (NHHC) A tug tows a camouflage float into position to protect *Tirpitz* in Fættenfjord, 1942. A German minesweeper is steaming by at right. (NHHC)

First Action

ADAPTED FROM "GERMAN ATTACKS ON THE MURMANSK RUN" BY A. E. SOKOL, U.S. NAVAL INSTITUTE *PROCEEDINGS*, DECEMBER 1952

By March 1942, the number and size of Allied convoys to northern Russia had increased to a point where they offered a tempting target for German attacks. Weather conditions also began to favor the attacker, as lengthening hours of daylight improved his chances of spotting a convoy and maintaining contact with it. In fact, from April to June the weather in that region is usually good, while the summer months are often foggy, which naturally reduces the Air Force's chances of successful attack. In winter, navigation in those waters is, of course, made exceedingly difficult by the combination of darkness, extreme cold, and the alternation between snowstorms and hurricanes, with icebergs and ice floes greatly adding to the dangers to which ships are exposed.

The North Russia convoys at that time assembled at Loch Ewe, on the west coast of Scotland; from there they first passed around Iceland, to enable escorting vessels to refuel, and then proceeded east, keeping as far north—and as far away from Norway—as the position of the polar ice-pack allowed. On that course they continued at least to the longitude of Murmansk before turning south. They were escorted by a force of British cruisers, destroyers, and corvettes, while a covering fleet of several battleships, at least one aircraft carrier, and a number of cruisers and destroyers was kept in readiness at sea, to go to the convoy's aid if necessary. As a rule, however, this task force was kept in the region between Bear Island and Jan Mayen, well outside the range of German land-based planes. Russia-bound convoys at that time bore the designation PQ, with the current

number, while the homeward-bound ones were called QP.

The first attack on these convoys was launched late in December 1941, by a few German destroyers, but it was beaten off by the naval escort. Between January and March 1942, three attacks were made by U-boats, and several merchant ships were sunk. But a large-scale operation was not attempted until the beginning of March 1942, when two convoys, PQ 12 and QP 8, were on their way simultaneously.

About noon, March 5, German air reconnaissance sighted a convoy of 15 ships, steering a north-easterly course and located 70 to 80 miles south of Jan Mayen. Thereupon, the German Air Force was ordered to attack, and six submarines were dispatched for the same purpose, although they were restricted to operations in the area east of 26 degrees East—the longitude of the North Cape—in order not to interfere with German surface ships.

Photographed from the battleship *Tirpitz*, the heavy cruiser *Admiral Hipper* is at right, two destroyers to the left. (NHHC)

At the same time, the battleship *Tirpitz* and three destroyers [*Hermann Schoemann, Friedrich Ihn*, and the larger, 5.9-in armed *Z25*] lying in Trondheim made ready for action. The task force was under the tactical command of Vice Admiral Ciliax, the Commander of Battleships, but the operational direction lay with the Naval Command, Group North, with headquarters in Kiel. At noon, March 6, the ships were instructed to proceed, at a speed of 25 knots, to a point halfway between Jan Mayen and Bear Island where, it was assumed, the convoy would be at about 1600 hours on March 7. The destroyers were to refuel from *Tirpitz* during the night. According to his orders, the task force commander was to avoid combat with superior forces, to accept a fight with those of equal strength only if necessary to achieve the main objective—the destruction of the convoy—but destroy inferior forces if that could be done without interfering with the main goal.

Vizeadmiral Ciliax did not entirely agree with these orders. He objected, first, to the late hour of starting the operation, which necessitated the high speed and the early refueling of the destroyers, cut down the time he would have to search for the convoy, and made easier an early discovery of his departure. Leaving the preceding night he could have, for a much longer time, escaped detection by enemy agents or British submarines watching the coast of Norway. Taking it for granted that the convoy would be protected by a force of heavy ships, even though German scouts had not spotted it as yet, he also argued that even a successful fight with such opponents might put *Tirpitz* out of commission for a long time. Only a task of major importance, not the attack on a single convoy, would justify such a risk. But assuming that the higher command had a much clearer picture of the overall situation than he had, he finally acquiesced.

THE SORTIE OF *TIRPITZ*

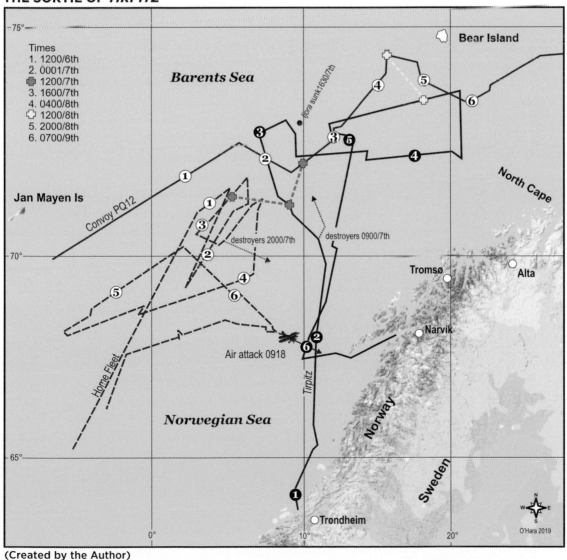

(Created by the Author)

Prinz Eugen, in company with *Admiral Scheer* and the destroyers *Beitzen, Jacobi, Ihn,* and *Z25,* and the torpedo boat *Seeadler*, left for Trondheim on 20 February. This time, however, the British were not caught napping. They had anticipated that more ships would be joining *Tirpitz*. Coastal Command was patrolling the North Sea and four submarines the waters off Trondheim. There the submarine *Trident* torpedoed *Prinz Eugen* on her approach to the fjord and blew off the ship's rudder and a portion of her stern. The rest of the squadron arrived safely. *Prinz Eugen* made port, but she would need to return to Germany for permanent repairs.

Tirpitz sailed from Trondheim at 1100 on 6 March escorted by four destroyers and two torpedo boats (that evening three of the escorts, *Jacobi, T5,* and *T12,* returned to Trondheim). They were barely at sea when *Seawolf*, one of the British submarines watching the exits to Trondheimfjord, spotted the squadron. She was unable to reach an attack position and at 1940 surfaced to radio a sighting. This news reached Admiral Tovey, the commander of the Home Fleet, at around midnight. Tovey had already sortied to cover the outward passage of PQ 12 and the inward passage of QP 8. He flew his flag in *King George V*, which sailed with the aircraft carrier *Victorious*, the heavy cruiser *Berwick*, and six destroyers. To the north and coming on a converging course was the battle cruiser *Renown*, the battleship *Duke of York*, and six destroyers.

During the morning of the 7th Ciliax detached his destroyers to sweep north along a line east of the battleship. Unbeknownst to the Germans, Tovey and the Home Fleet (the two sections had united) were steaming northeast on a converging course. In fact, had the British held their course, they would have crossed ahead of *Tirpitz* that morning. Instead, Tovey turned north and then southwest. He had sent his destroyers to refuel and wanted to reduce his heavy ships' exposure to German submarines. By noon *Tirpitz* was about 90 miles southsouthwest of the convoy and about the same distance east-southeast of Tovey, who was still steaming away. Despite their proximity both admirals were operating in the dark. Ciliax had no idea the Home Fleet was at sea, much less in his near proximity, while the weather was keeping *Victorious* from sending scouts aloft and clearly affecting German aerial reconnaissance.

At 1628, after a long run north, *Ihn* found *Ijora*, a Russian straggler from QP 8, and sank her. Tovey picked up the distress signal but was not sure of the ship's location. At 1650 he turned east-southeast. He then received "Ultra" information that *Tirpitz* was heading north, so he altered course in that direction. He also sent six destroyers to search to the east along the enemy's presumed route of return. Nothing was found, as *Tirpitz* was to the north searching for the convoy. By nightfall, the German battleship was roughly 80 miles east of PQ 12 and west of PQ 8. Ciliax collected his destroyers and attempted to refuel them that night, but conditions were too rough, and at 2013 on the 7th he sent *Ihn* to Harstad. At 0640 the next morning emptying bunkers forced *Z25* and *Schoemann* to make for Tromsø.

On the 8th Ciliax sailed west and then turned due north at dawn and headed toward Bear Island. By this time he was between PQ 12 and its destination, but German reconnaissance failed him again. He exchanged signals with a FW 200 Condor reconnaissance aircraft at noon when the convoy was only 70 miles northwest of his position. This was a parlous moment for the British. Tovey had concluded that *Tirpitz* had given up the hunt and was now far to the southwest and sailing in the wrong direction. His report explained that he was heading for Iceland "to collect some destroyers." But fortune and the weather favored the British: *Tirpitz*, aircraft, and submarines saw nothing of the convoy. In the words of the German SKL War Diary, "The operation did not achieve the desired result on 8 Mar." At 2025 on the 8th Ciliax concluded that conditions did not justify the continued risk to the battleship and so turned south by west to rendezvous with his escort off Vestfjord before returning to base.

At 1820 Tovey had come about and shaped a course to the northeast. This was because a series of signals told him that *Tirpitz* had been hunting the convoy this entire time and specified where and when she was to rendezvous with her destroyers. At 0243 *Victorious* turned southeast and began a run in toward Vestfjord, where she hoped to be able to launch an airstrike against *Tirpitz* the next morning. The strike aircraft embarked on *Victorious* were of the Fairey Albacore type, biplane torpedo/dive-bomber/spotter-reconnaissance aircraft. At 0640 Tovey ordered the carrier to fly off six of her 18 Albacores to search ahead for the battleship. At 0735 a strike force of a dozen Albacores armed with 18-inch Mk XV torpedoes and commanded by Lt. Cdr. W. J. Lucas, followed. At 0802 one of the reconnaissance aircraft spotted *Tirpitz* and *Ihn,* her sole escort, off Vestfjord. The battleship launched two of her Arado Ar 196s, which attacked the shadowing aircraft, but

HMS *Victorious* receiving a Fairey Albatross torpedo bomber. (NHHC)

the strike force picked up Tirpitz at 0842 on ASV radar at a range of 16 miles.

The Albacore could do no better than 100 knots burdened with their heavy loads; *Tirpitz* was steaming at 29 knots into a headwind of 35 knots. This meant the Albacores closed the enemy at only 35–40 knots. In these circumstances, and given the heavy antiaircraft barrage the ship's batteries were throwing into the path of the aircraft, Lucas felt there was no alternative but to order his subflights to attack independently rather than position the flights for a coordinated attack, which required them to pull well ahead of the battleship and simultaneously attack from the port and starboard bow.

At 0917 the first flight of three aircraft drew up alongside the battleship's port beam and swung to starboard to drop weapons from about 3,000 yards. *Tirpitz*, with ample time to react, swung hard to port, and the torpedoes missed well astern. The second subflight launched its Mk XVs, set to run at a depth of 25 feet and a speed of 40 knots, at a range of about 2,000 yards, also on the port side; these also missed astern. The

second pair of subflights attacked the battleship from the starboard side at 0925. As *Tirpitz* swung to starboard, her weapons shot down two of the attackers in the act of releasing their weapons. Three of the four remaining torpedoes missed astern, but the fourth passed behind the ship with only a dozen yards to spare.

In their analysis of the action the Admiralty blamed the commander, Lucas, who had just joined *Victorious* and had never flown with its air group before, for the failure. He had not practiced a torpedo attack since 1937, and the rest of his men had little training in coordinated attacks on enemy capital ships. The official British history is a little kinder noting that "the rapid expansion of the Fleet Air Arm then in progress made it inevitable that its squadrons should be constantly diluted by semi-trained crews." Flying a slow aircraft that was unsuited for the conditions was, however, the biggest reason for the failure.

Although *Tirpitz* returned safely to port, the operation did influence the battleship's future as her narrow escape made the German navy even more reluctant to risk its most powerful individual asset.

First Action

ADAPTED FROM "GERMAN ATTACKS ON THE MURMANSK RUN,"
BY A. E. SOKOL, U.S. NAVAL INSTITUTE *PROCEEDINGS*, DECEMBER 1952

The negative result [of the sortie against Convoy PQ 12] led the German Naval High Command to conclude:

> Its course shows the weakness of our naval situation in the northern area. The enemy responds to every German move by dispatching strong forces, especially aircraft carriers, which must be considered the most dangerous opponent of our heavy ships! It is characteristic of our extremely weak defense that the enemy dares to

advance into the coastal waters of the northern area without being annihilated by the German Air Force. Our own defensive forces (destroyers and torpedo boats) are so few in number that our ships are in gravest danger whenever they are exposed to air attacks or come into contact with enemy naval forces.

The War Diary also notes the experience gained regarding the enemy's behavior:

> Opponent operates very skillfully—completely unobtrusive use of radio, very effective shadowing by planes, ruthless and daring attacks by torpedo bomb-

After her March sortie *Tirpitz* spent most of her time sheltering at her berth in Fættenfjord. The greatest activity of her crew was changing the camouflage. (NHHC)

ers, operationally correct use of submarines, extremely effective employment of forces by all commanders involved, as well as elastic direction of the convoy (immediate change of course when sighted by us), splendid cooperation between sea and air forces.

It proceeds to draw the following lessons from these conditions:

(a) Absolute prerequisite to any successful operation in the Northern Sea, in the absence of an aircraft carrier of our own, is strong support by our Air Force in the Norway area (including reconnaissance, fighters, torpedo planes);

(b) In view of the resolute reaction by the enemy, any operation in the Northern Sea requires the employment of all our naval forces, especially as long as there are aircraft carriers available to the enemy;

(c) It is therefore desirable that our naval forces be held back for the time being, in order to have them ready to repulse enemy landing attempts. They should at present be employed only if our reconnaissance has furnished accurate information about the enemy and if there is adequate support by our Air Force;

(d) It must be categorically demanded that the Air Force wage relentless warfare against enemy carri-

ers. Their elimination at sea or at their bases must be the supreme objective of our Air Force's [contribution to] naval war in the northern area. Their extermination would constitute a radical improvement of our operational possibilities;

(e) We must demand that work on our own aircraft carrier be accelerated. This includes also the provision of an adequate number of carrier planes. The early formation of a German task force composed of *Tirpitz*, *Scharnhorst*, a carrier, two heavy cruisers, and 12 to 14 destroyers must be attempted at all costs. It would represent a grave danger to the enemy in the northern area and would be capable of carrying out important and successful operations.

Hitler agreed with *Großadmiral* Raeder that the heavy ships should not be exposed to danger without air reconnaissance and protection. But even so, Raeder obtained Luftwaffe cooperation only with difficulty. The Navy and the Air Force had long fought for the control of naval air forces: the deadlock was never completely resolved and prevented proper coordination of plans as well as smooth cooperation in carrying them out. Yet the following months showed clearly enough what effective cooperation between the two services could achieve.

FLEET IN BEING

APRIL–SEPTEMBER 1942

At midnight on 12 March *Tirpitz* departed Narvik and set out for Trondheim. She arrived at 2100 on 13 March and anchored in Fættenfjord. The Royal Navy's Fleet Air Arm had missed an excellent opportunity to destroy *Tirpitz*, in part because it was still, after two and a half years of war, flying inadequate aircraft manned by inexperienced personnel in its most important frontline unit—a fruit of the general indifference to and distrust of carrier warfare of the Royal Air Force, from which the Fleet Air Arm had been returned to Admiralty control only in 1939. The British in general and Admiral Tovey in particular were still learning how best to use the intelligence gained by their ability to read certain types

Tirpitz at her protected berth in Fættenfjord. (Peter Schenk Collection)

Hampton Halifax bomber. (Public Domain)

Dancers entertain the crewmen on the battleship's after deck, moored in Fættenfjord in the summer of 1942. Note the camouflage hung on the ship's 38-cm gun turrets. (NHHC)

of German radio traffic. If handled in accordance with its best intelligence, the Home Fleet could have intercepted *Tirpitz* with battleships rather than staking all its hopes on a dozen, slow, biwing torpedo bombers. The whole episode offered a disquieting snapshot of the British navy at war.

Tirpitz in Trondheim remained an effective fleet in being, in fact more effective than before because the Germans had demonstrated a willingness actually to use her. This, combined with his fixation on the battleship's potential, caused Churchill to push the RAF to attack the ship, despite the difficulties of the mission and the low probability of success. The RAF refused to send its unescorted heavy bombers into the teeth of the German air defense (the RAF estimated there were a hundred fighters based in the Trondheim area) in daylight; it would only conduct missions at night. There were only a few nights a month with sufficient moonlight for the bombers to find their targets. These missions also, of course, required good weather. Thus, the next raid did not occur until 30/31 March, when 34 Halifax bombers attacked. *Tirpitz* was covered with camouflage, making her hard to spot from the air. Cliffs that soared above her enclosed anchorage made her difficult to approach. The final straw was thick chemical smoke that billowed over the ship as the attackers approached. Only one Halifax succeeded in dropping its bombs—none landed close enough to damage the ship—and five failed to return. The pilot of one of the lost aircraft later remembered, "I was hit fairly frequently before I reached the coast and was a flamer before I got to *Tirpitz*. I saw her masts sticking out of the smoke as we went over, then the starboard wing folded up. I got out just in time. My chute opened just before I hit the snow." He avoided capture and hiked to Sweden. Another crewman wrote, "We went down to forty feet, the flak was coming both down at us and up at us. I was firing at cliffs and boats as we went by. Then the skipper said here's the *Tirpitz* now, and I went berserk on the guns, and sprayed the *Tirpitz* from stem to stern. The skipper shouted out, we've been hit, I'll try and get her over the mountain, which he did, and we landed on a frozen lake."

During the next full moon, at the end of April, the British dispatched two attacks. On 27/28 April 29 Halifax and 11 Lancasters struck in two waves, the Lancasters first from high altitude followed by the Halifaxes coming in low. Thirty-two aircraft found the target and dropped 94 bombs through the smoke, including twenty 4,000-lb weapons. None fell close enough to do any damage, and five bombers were shot down or otherwise lost. The next night 23 Halifax and 11 Lancasters again attacked. Some of these carried mines that were supposed to roll down the steep slope beside the ship and explode beneath her. Foiled once again by smoke, they blindly dropped 90 bombs or mines and scored no hits. Two Halifaxs did not return.

Rest and Recreation

Tirpitz spent most of her career at anchor in isolated, even wild, settings far from the types of recreational opportunities that sailors normally relish. Maintaining crew morale in such conditions was a challenge, one not always successfully met. At Fættenfjord there was skiing in the winter and, with the coming of spring, fishing and hiking. The Germans requisitioned a nearby island that had holiday cabins and turned it into a rest camp called "Tipito." Small groups of men from each of the ship's 12 divisions could rest there for several days at a time. The camp had an open-air theater where the ship's band gave concerts. Camp rules were strict and forbade campfires, hunting, picking plants or flowers, or gathering eggs. Nonetheless, a black market quickly developed. The Germans traded tobacco and alcohol with local Norwegians for fresh food and eggs. The men also smuggled girls onto the island for parties. This rest area lasted until the Trondheim commander heard about the girls whereupon he closed it. The impact of isolation and solitude on the crew was shown by one case when an 18-year-old crewman deserted. Recaptured near the Swedish border, he said he had jumped ship because he was bored and planned to volunteer for service on a merchantman so he could see some action. He was tried for treason and shot by a firing squad made up of his division mates. This incident hardly helped morale.

Crewman putting the finishing touches on a fine model of the ship. Apparently, the crew had leisure time for such activities. (NHHC)

During the winter and spring of 1942, the Germans repeatedly attacked Allied convoys to Murmansk. They had failed to gain any decisive victories using surface warships, but their pressure was growing, and with the coming of the long days of summer and the accumulation of enough fuel oil to permit operations by the large ships, it seemed to the German naval command that an opportunity to employ the powerful fleet gathered in Norway would soon arrive. On 1 June staff started working on a plan called "Operation Rösselsprung." The intention was to intercept a Murmansk convoy using all the navy's surface assets, except that after *Tirpitz'* close call three months before, restrictions had been placed on the use of the large warships and Hitler's express consent was required before *Tirpitz* could sail. At a conference with Hitler on 17 June 1942 Raeder raised the question of attacking PQ 17, which was then gathering in Iceland. Hitler gave permission for the navy to concentrate in the far north but reiterated his basic concern, that he considered aircraft carriers "a great threat to the large vessels. The aircraft carriers must be located before the attack, and they must be rendered harmless by our Ju88 planes before the attack gets under way." The naval task force could not sortie until Hitler gave approval. At this time after successful carrier actions at Taranto against Italian battleships, at Pearl Harbor against American battleships, and *Tirpitz'* near-run affair in March (not to mention *Bismarck's* misfortunes with British carriers), the Führer had become a strong (if temporary) advocate of aircraft carriers. He had ordered the German navy's own first carrier, *Graf Zeppelin*, which had been languishing incomplete since spring 1940, to be finished. He has also ordered the almost complete heavy cruiser *Seidlitz* to be converted to a light carrier. Studies to convert three liners to carriers were also under way.

The Arctic Convoys

ADAPTED FROM "GERMAN ATTACKS ON THE MURMANSK RUN,"
BY A. E. SOKOL, U.S. NAVAL INSTITUTE *PROCEEDINGS*, DECEMBER 1952

The next attack by surface ships [against an Allied Murmansk convoy] occurred on March 28, when a group of three German destroyers tangled with PQ 13. As snow squalls hid the opponents from each other to the last moment, the Germans came upon the convoy suddenly; in the ensuing fight the escorting cruiser, H.M.S. *Trinidad*, and the destroyer *Eclipse* were torpedoed, and one German [ship] was sunk. With the protective screen thus weakened, the convoy became the prey of the German bombers and U-boats, which attacked it despite the prevailing dirty weather. The furious onslaught continued even after the ships had reached Murmansk, only 70 miles from the German air base at Petsamo. Several steamers were lost on this run; *Trinidad*, though badly damaged, managed to reach port and was quickly repaired. But a few weeks later, when escorting another convoy, she was bombed from the air and sank.

Although the Germans seemed to concentrate on the Russia-bound convoys, they did not entirely overlook the homeward-bound ones. On April 28, QP 11 left Murmansk, consisting of 13 steamers, H.M. cruiser *Edinburgh*, eight destroyers, six corvettes, and one armed trawler, that is, more escorting vessels than merchantmen.

QP 11 was attacked on May 1 by three German destroyers which were, however, prevented from closing in on the convoy by the skillful maneuvering of the escorting force. After a fight of four hours' duration, the Germans were forced to withdraw because they were running out of ammunition. In the meantime, the convoy commander had taken his charges into the ice, where they remained for seven or eight hours and whither the destroyers could not follow on account of their thin plates.

During the fighting, the escorting cruiser, H.M.S. *Edinburgh*, had been attacked and damaged by two U-boats. The retreating German destroyers made an attempt to finish her off with torpedoes, but they found to their surprise that the cruiser's fire power had not been diminished by her injury. In fact, the defense put up by her and the protecting four destroyers was so effective that one of the German vessels was hit and had to be abandoned by her crew. Unfortunately, *Edinburgh* also had to be sunk on her way home.

While QP 11 escaped without the loss of any of the merchant ships, the east-bound PQ 15, consisting of 23 ships, at sea at the same time, had worse luck. Continually attacked by German planes for 48 hours, it suffered considerable damage. On the other hand, the next returning convoy, QP 12, which left Murmansk on May 21, again got through without any losses.

The unsuccessful destroyer attacks had showed the German Naval High Command that the employment of these units, unprotected by heavy ships, could only lead to losses out of proportion to the results achieved. Yet the period from April to June had offered no favorable

In Operation *Rösselsprung* the Germans intended to deploy two groups:

- Trondheim Group, consisting of *Tirpitz* (flying the flag of *Vizeadmiral* Otto Schniewind), *Hipper*, and the destroyers *Ihn*, *Lody*, *Galster*, *Riedel*, *Eckoldt*, and *Steinbrinck* (the last four to be transferred from Germany to Trondheim).

- Narvik Group, consisting of *Lützow*, *Admiral Scheer*, and destroyers *Z24*, *Z27*, *Z28*, *Z29*, *Z30*, and *Beitzen*, all under *Vizeadmiral* Oskar Kummetz.

When Convoy PQ 17 was located, Group North gave permission for the Trondheim Group to take station at the northern exit of Altafjord and meet there the Narvik Group. Together they would intercept and destroy the convoy. The escort was to be engaged only if "indispensable for accomplishing the main task." *Tirpitz* and *Hipper* would deal with the escort while *Lützow* and *Scheer* focused on the convoy. There were the usual caveats: "An engagement with superior enemy forces is to be avoided. The operation should be executed quickly; and should be completed before an enemy security unit composed of battleships and carriers . . . has a chance to intervene. . . . The operation will be executed only if reconnaissance has established with certainty that there is no risk of becoming involved with superior enemy forces."

Although the Germans anticipated that PQ 17 would sail in June, in the event it was delayed because the Home Fleet had to divert forces to the Mediterranean to escort a convoy to Malta. This delay showed the great stresses on the British navy; having suffered the loss of five battleships in November and December 1941, it was no longer capable of conducting simultaneous major convoy operations in the Arctic and Mediterranean, even with help from the U.S. Navy.

opportunity for the use of the heavy surface ships. Air reconnaissance had not furnished sufficient information about convoys and their covering forces to warrant another sortie by the *Tirpitz* and the cruisers. The critical fuel situation alone forbade a thrust into an uncertain and therefore risky position.

But even so, by the middle of April 1942, the North Cape route had become so dangerous that the British were unable to provide enough escorts for the convoys. Sixteen out of 84 northbound ships and 11 out of 78 southbound ships, in four convoys each way, had been sunk, not including serious damage suffered in Murmansk itself. These losses were far greater than those on any other route. In Reykjavik there were dozens of ships awaiting the formation of a convoy, others had to turn back from the Murmansk run, still others had to be routed to Scotland instead of Iceland because of the congestion in Reykjavik. At the same time, the Russians pressed for quicker delivery of the badly-needed weapons and ammunition. To relieve the British Navy, the United States sent Task Force 39, under the command of Rear Admiral John W. Wilcox, Jr. It included our two newest battleships, the *Washington* and *North Carolina*, the aircraft carrier *Wasp*, the heavy cruisers *Wichita* and *Tuscaloosa*, and Destroyer Squadron 8. Task Force 39 stayed until the worst danger had passed.

At Scapa Flow, April 1942. In the foreground is USS *Wasp* (CV 7). In the background are (l–r): a *King George V*-class battleship, *Victorious*, *Washington* (BB 56), and *Wichita* (CA 45). (NHHC)

PQ 17 consisted of 35 ships with a multilayered escort: The "immediate escort" was three minesweepers and four trawlers. The "close escort" had six Hunt-type small destroyers, four corvettes, two submarines, two antiaircraft ships, and three rescue vessels. The "close escort support group" had four heavy cruisers (two American) and three destroyers (two American). Finally, the "heavy support group," under Admiral John Tovey, had the battleships *Duke of York* and USS *Washington*, the carrier *Victorious*, a heavy cruiser, a light cruiser, and 14 destroyers. As early as 18 June the British naval attaché in Stockholm had passed along to London the essentials of the German plan. Ultra confirmed that this information was "wheat," not "chaff." Tovey recommended that PQ 17 be deferred until more ships were available for the escort. The First Sea Lord, Admiral Dudley Pound, agreed. However, given the defeats being suffered by the Soviets that summer, political necessity overruled military logic. The convoy had to sail. The fact he had lost cruisers in the last two operations especially worried Pound; he told Tovey that if the admiral believed the convoy faced destruction from a superior enemy surface force, he could order it to scatter. Tovey replied that he considered this would be "sheer, bloody murder."

The merchant ships departed Hvalfjord on 27 June. Radio intelligence gave the Germans a rough idea of the convoy's progress, and the first contact occurred on 1 July, when the escort drove off two German submarines. On 2 July aircraft unsuccessfully attacked the convoy.

On 2 July at 2000 *Tirpitz* departed Trondheim in company with *Admiral Hipper*, the destroyers *Glaster*, *Ihn*, *Lody*, and *Riedel*, and torpedo boats *T7* and *T15*. They were bound for Gimsöy on Vestfjord and ultimately Altafjord to rendezvous with the battle group from Narvik under *Vizeadmiral* Oskar Kummetz. Kummetz, flying his flag on *Lützow*, led *Admiral Scheer* and the destroyers *Z24*, *Z27*, *Z28*, *Z29*, and *Z30* from Narvik at 2400 on the 2nd. The German commanders and crews were in high spirits, glad to have their routines broken and anxious to play an active role in the war.

Matters of intelligence dominated events over the next two days. The Germans sighted the convoy and its support force, but—given naval staff's requirement for absolute clarity on British positions—this information did not really help. The German Naval Staff War Diary for 3 July summarized the situation as follows:

> Beginning at 0105 air reconnaissance again located the escort force in quadrant AB 7893, consisting of 1 carrier, 1 battleship and 2 cruisers proceeding on an easterly course and another force consisting of 1 carrier, 2 battleships, 3 cruisers, and 5 destroyers in quadrant AF 1621, on the same course. Group North is of the opinion that both formations constitute a single group, although it is not impossible that 2 separate groups might be following the convoy, in an easterly direction. No reports came in concerning these escort groups between 0430 and 2240. At 2240 a force consisting of 1 battleship, 3 heavy cruisers and 3 destroyers was reported by air reconnaissance in quadrant AB 3943, hence in the immediate vicinity of the convoy. It still remains to be ascertained whether these vessels have been correctly identified. It is possible that the report concerns the cruiser and destroyer escorts directly assigned to the convoy, while the report of the presence of a battleship is the result of erroneous identification."

In fact, Group North was right. The first sighting at 0105 had placed Tovey's force. The second sighting was wrong. There was only one carrier out there.

In addition to uncertainties about the enemy fleet's location, the Germans were suffering subtractions from their own force as the squadrons moved to their deployment areas. First, *Lützow*, sailing in thick fog, struck a rock in Tjeld Sound at 0245 on the 3rd. The damage was serious, and Kummetz had to transfer his flag to *Scheer*. Then, *Galster*, *Riedel*, and *Lody* all, according to the Staff War Diary, "scraped bottom" at around 1700 the same day on an uncharted shoal after running up Vestfjord and entering Gimsöy. Despite such losses, the operation continued.

Schniewind expected to receive orders from Group North to head for Altafjord immediately, but the German command was still trying to update the location of the British battleships and carrier. After four hours the impatient admiral decided to sail on his own initiative. Meanwhile, again in the words of the Naval Staff War Diary, "The Führer could temporarily not be reached but Vice Admiral Krancke [naval liaison at Führer headquarters] felt sure that, on the basis of

Photographed from the battleship *Tirpitz*. The next ship is the heavy cruiser *Admiral Hipper*, followed by *Admiral Scheer* and several destroyers and torpedo boats. (NHHC)

Photographed from the battleship *Tirpitz*. The next ship is the heavy cruiser *Admiral Hipper*, followed by the *Admiral Scheer* and several destroyers and torpedo boats. (NHHC)

PQ 17 forming off the west coast of Iceland, late June 1942. (NHHC)

information which he had previously imparted to the Führer, no objection to the transfer of the ships to Altafjord would be made by him. Therefore the Chief of Staff, Naval Staff [Raeder], instructed the Commanding Admiral, Group North by telephone to transfer the ships as proposed."

Schniewind was already under way when he finally received permission to sail. At 1030 on the 4th *Tirpitz*, *Hipper*, and *Ihn* joined *Scheer* and her five destroyers at Altafjord. At this time the convoy was east of Bear Island and directly north of North Cape. It had been only lightly attacked and had suffered no casualties. In London, however, the situation appeared dire, at least to Admiral Pound. News arrived on the 3rd that *Tirpitz*

had left Trondheim, but there was no indication where she had gone. On the morning of the 4th, Pound met with his staff to discuss the threatening situation. The meeting lasted most of the day, and as more information trickled in the First Sea Lord felt impelled to intervene directly in the tactical situation, as when he directly radioed the cruiser commander giving him permission to go farther east than planned.

Meanwhile, the German admirals were pondering improbabilities of their own. The intelligence picture on the 4th was not positive.

A convoy escort force composed of 1 battleship, 2 heavy cruisers and 3 destroyers was spotted at

---

The Soviet Attack on Tirpitz

"REPORT OF THE COMMANDER AND COMMISSAR OF *K-21* OF THE NORTHERN FLEET ON COMBAT OPERATIONS OF THE SUBMARINE IN THE PERIOD FROM 18 JUNE TO 9 JULY 1942," TRANSLATED BY STEPHEN MCLAUGHLIN

At 1633 on 5 July 1942 the hydrophone operators reported a sound on the starboard bow to the watch commander; the [watch commander] set course toward the sound, but nothing was observed through the periscope, and only when it was raised for the second time was an enemy submarine seen on the surface at a range of 40–50 cables [8,000 to 10,000 yards]. Taking control, when the periscope was raised I established that this was [indeed] a submarine, and, having grasped the situation, I began to maneuver for an attack. At 1712 it was established that two torpedo boats were coming out to sea at high speed; at the same time we realized that we had mistaken another torpedo boat for a submarine—refraction had somewhat raised up the tips of the funnel and bridges; I continued the attack on the second echelon that was steaming behind the torpedo boat.

At 1718 I observed the mast-tops of a large ship, sailing in line abreast with the escorting torpedo boats. The leading torpedo boats, evidently scouting the area, sailed toward us at distances of 50–20 cables [10,000 to 4,000 yards], turned around and went off to approach the squadron. I set course for an attack, taking as a target the one steaming to the left of us.

At 1723 I identified the enemy ships steaming in company with two battleships—"Tirpitz" and probably "Scheer," protected by eight torpedo boats of the "Karl Galster" type, moving in a complex zigzag.

"Arado" type aircraft provided air patrols above the squadron. I began to maneuver for an attack on the battleship "Tirpitz" with the bow [torpedo tubes].

At 1736 the squadron turned together to port by 90–100°, taking up a line ahead formation with a distance of 20–30 cables [4,000 to 6,000 yards] between the battleships. The submarine was moving away on the opposite course; we swung to starboard on the bow [torpedo tubes].

At. 1750 the entire squadron again turned together and the battleship "Tirpitz" was now steaming toward the sub with her course 5–7° on the port side. Fearing that my attack would be frustrated, we brought the stern torpedo tubes to bear and at 1801 fired a four-torpedo spread with a 4-second interval between torpedoes, with ranges of the salvo being 20–17–18 cables [4,000–3,400–3,600 yards], . . . estimating the speed of the battleship to be 22 knots and ourselves moving at 3.5 knots.

At the moment we [fired] the salvo we were located approximately in the middle of the squadron, the battleship "Scheer" had already passed beyond the firing angle and was on my starboard side, inside the four zigzagging torpedo boats, [when] the leading torpedo boat that was protecting the battleship "Tirpitz" turned sharply to port on an opposite course and I feared that he was moving toward the submarine. When the first torpedo was launched I lowered the periscope and when the last torpedo was launched I drove the boat deep and increased to full speed.

After 3 minutes 15 seconds by stopwatch two torpedo explosions were reported from the compartments and also by the acoustics [hydrophone operators?]. The sound of the torpedo boat first approached, then moved off. The

---

1327 by submarine TJ "457" in quadrant AC 1542, proceeding eastward. This convoy was reported in the same strength by submarines and planes until 2145. The escort forces kept at a distance of 60 to 90 miles north of the convoy. It was last located by a plane at 2145, some 200 miles northeast of Bear Island. The report does not state whether it was still on an easterly course or going west. The force which had been reported by air reconnaissance at 1201 in quadrant AC 1548, said to consist of 1 heavy British cruiser and 3 heavy American cruisers as well as 1 British and 2 American destroyers, may be assumed to be the immediate escort of the convoy. No carriers were spotted, although judging from the presence of 2 torpedo bombers, reported by air shadower at 1832, there is a likelihood that one is in the vicinity.

Staff concluded that the presence of a heavy enemy force in the convoy's vicinity made it impossible to seek an engagement. Thus, the German fleet swung on short cables at three hours' notice. Raeder set a deadline for ordering a sortie: 1700 on the 5th. On the evening of the 4th, however, news began to arrive of successful submarine and air attacks against PQ 17.

In the convoy itself the escort had broken up several air attacks, and confidence was high. At 1000 on the 4th Tovey and the heavy escort was about 200 miles

expected explosions of depth charges never came, and only at 1831 did we hear gradually diminishing rolling explosions lasting up to 20 seconds, followed by [more explosions] at 1832 and 1838; these did not resemble the explosions of individual depth charges.

I consider it probable that "Tirpitz" was hit by two torpedoes, [but] this could not be confirmed by intelligence; at the same time one must admit the possibility that the leading torpedo boat, which was turning at the moment of the [torpedo] shots onto the opposite course from the battleship, intercepted the torpedoes herself; in favor of this suggestion is the evidence of the subsequent large explosions.

I do not understand why the escort ships did not pursue the boat after a four-torpedo salvo. One may suggest that, due to the fear of a screen from the sub [?], the torpedo boats, having failed to observe the sub before the salvo, did not receive an order to pursue it from the battleship.

The Soviet submarine *K21*. She claimed two hits on *Tirpitz*. (Boris Lemachko Collection)

northwest of Bear Island sailing east. Like Pound, Tovey was awaiting news of *Tirpitz*.

It was taking roughly 12 hours to break the German naval codes at this point. On the evening of the 4th the Admiralty received an intercept of a message generated at 0740 that morning by Schniewind to Kummetz stating that he would be arriving at Altafjord at 0900 with *Tirpitz*. From this Admiral Pound, aware that the German plan was proceeding and knowing the forces at the enemy's disposal, calculated that in the worse possible case the German fleet could even at that moment be closing the convoy. Against the advice of his intelligence officer and most of his staff, Pound ordered the close escort to head west (at 2111) and the convoy to disperse (2123) and then to scatter (2136). These instructions flabbergasted the British (and Americans) all up and down the line of command. The commander of the close escort later wrote, "[These orders] led me to believe that not only were they [the Admiralty] in possession of later information but that *Tirpitz* was at sea and in the near vicinity of the convoy." The convoy commodore reached the same conclusion. "We were all expecting therefore, to see either the cruisers open fire, or to see enemy masts appearing over the horizon."

The escort duly retreated, and the convoy duly scattered. Up until that point the convoy had lost three ships with one damaged. Over the next day a dozen ships would be sunk; ultimately, of the 35 that set out for Murmansk, only 11 would arrive. As Tovey had predicted, it was indeed sheer, bloody murder.

At 0655 on the 5th a German aircraft, quite by accident, spotted the Home Fleet 200 miles northwest of Bear Island. This put it 800 miles from the possible point of action, so Group North asked Raeder for permission to dispatch *Tirpitz*. Raeder relayed the request to Führer headquarters, where Krancke was able to speak to Hitler. Hitler said yes. Krancke told Raeder, Raeder told Group North, and Group North gave Schniewind the permission he had been seeking for two days and had finally despaired of getting. At 1130 *Tirpitz*, *Scheer*, *Hipper*, and nine destroyers set sail. By 1500 they were well into the Barents Sea.

They were not at sea long, however, before Allied units sighted them. First was the Russian submarine *K-21*. She fired four torpedoes and went deep. Based on two explosions heard, she claimed two hits. In fact, the Germans were unaware they had been attacked. More importantly, *K-21* surfaced after a half-hour and broadcast a sighting report. This was followed by a report at 1816 from a Coastal Command Catalina operating out of Russia. Finally, at 2059 the British

A German submarine torpedoing a barrage-balloon-carrying steamship from PQ 17. Photographed from the submarine. (NHHC)

UNITED STATES NAVAL INSTITUTE

U-boat crew on board their boat, at Narvik, Norway, following the action against PQ 17, flying a flag for every victim. Note 20-mm gun on conning tower, raised periscope, and antitorpedo nets in background. (NHHC)

submarine *P54* spotted *Tirpitz*. An aircraft drove her under, and she was unable to attack. It did not matter. The Germans deciphered these reports. Knowing that the convoy had scattered and receiving reports of successful air and submarine attacks, Raeder decided there was no point in continuing the operation. At 2130 Schniewind received orders to come about.

Tirpitz was back in Altafjord early on the 6th. At 1800 that day she departed for Narvik, arriving there on the 7th. The battleship had been at sea for only ten hours. She never came within hundreds of miles of the enemy, yet, her sortie against PQ 17 was one of the most successful naval operations of the war. Not only were two dozen ships sunk—largely because of the order to scatter—the German battleship had caused a slowdown on the critical convoy route at a time when it was still the major source of supply to the Soviet Union and the Soviets were under intense pressure from the German summer offensive toward the Volga and the Caucasus oil fields. The political ramifications were far greater than the military consequences of the sunken merchant ships.

Großadmiral Raeder visits German naval forces at Narvik, circa 1942. Raeder is in the front row, center. (NHHC)

QUEEN OF THE NORTH

OCTOBER 1942–SEPTEMBER 1943

On 8 July the German fleet anchored in Bogen Bay, near Narvik, and stayed there awaiting another opportunity to act against a convoy. However, after the PQ 17 disaster the Allies suspended sailing convoys to North Russia until September, when shorter daylight hours would offer better conditions for the defense.

Naval command began planning to bring *Tirpitz* back to Germany for a refit, scheduling it to take place at the Deutsche Werke yard in Kiel from the end of October 1942 through January 1943. In early September the ship's no. 2 diesel-electric engine was acting up and limiting her speed to 27 knots. At the same time, intelligence about PQ 18, the next Allied convoy operation, began to stir interest in Group North. They wanted to include *Tirpitz* in plans for intercepting this convoy, but Führer headquarters refused. Then, on 11 September, when discussing *Tirpitz*' refit, Hitler "demanded, if at all possible" that the ship not be sent to Germany for shipyard overhaul. Naval staff agreed to investigate doing the work, at least an overhaul of the engines, in Trondheim. On 23 October 1942, in Operation *Globus I*, *Tirpitz*, *Scheer*, and the destroyers *Eckoldt*, *Beitzen*, *Z23*, *Z28*, and *Z29* departed Narvik for Trondheim. They arrived the next day. *Tirpitz* began her refit, while *Scheer* and *Z28* continued to Germany.

Meanwhile, the great disaster suffered by the British navy at Alexandria, Egypt, in December 1941 when six Italian frogmen penetrated the harbor and severely damaged two battleships, a tanker, and a destroyer with explosive charges, intrigued some of the Admiralty's creative thinkers. On a different occasion, the British had captured one of the torpedo-like sleds the Italians had used to transport their explosive charges and basically copied it. By mid-1942 they had developed a plan to transport two of these devices ("chariots" in British usage, which was more inspiring than the Italian nickname, which translated to "pig" and was a reference to their handling characteristics) to Norway in a fishing boat with forged papers. The boat would bring the operators to within range of *Tirpitz* to make a sneak attack. On 26 October, after a period of training and preparation, this fishing boat, *Arthur*, left the Shetland Islands for Trondheim with two chariots on deck. The plan was for the trawler to lower the chariots once in Norwegian waters and tow them to the launch point.

Arthur made landfall on the 27th. There were delays, caused by unanticipated enemy aircraft patrols,

Italian SLC (*siluro a lunga corsa*). The British chariots used against *Tirpitz* were basically copies of this device. (F. Harrauer)

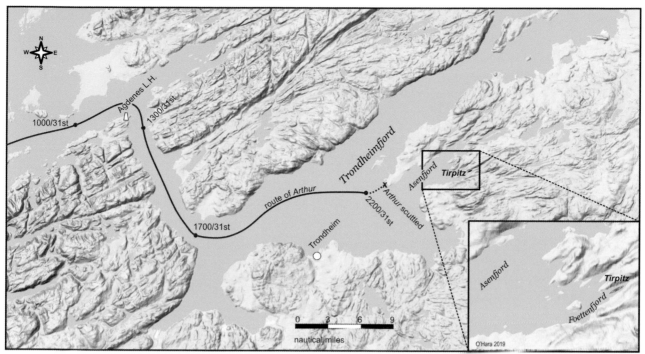

(Created by the Author)

friendly and curious fishermen, weather, and engine problems, but by the morning of the 30th the trawler was proceeding slowly up Trondheimfjord with the submerged chariots following behind at the end of a line. The first test came when *Arthur* arrived at the German examination boat that had to approve of all civilian traffic on the fjord.

What happened next is well described in Gervis Frere-Cook's *Attacks on the* Tirpitz, published by the Naval Institute Press in 1973, as the eighth in its "Sea Battles in Close-Up" series:

> The examination passed off successfully though not without apprehension. Everything was in order except the weather: a flat calm and bright sunshine left the chariots clearly visible below *Arthur*'s keel when she lay stopped, something which had not been foreseen back at [base]. A slight fracas with a heaving line distracted the attention of the German sailors as the two boats came close together and the chariots remained unnoticed for the quarter of an hour that the examining officer took with Larsen [the Norwegian acting as the fishing boat's skipper], checking the forged papers and enquiring about a colleague doing a like task further down the fjord. Eventually *Arthur* was permitted to proceed, her wake concealing the chariots from further observations.

Arthur continued without trouble for the rest of the forenoon and all afternoon up the fjord toward Trondheim, east-north-east to the Agdenes lighthouse, then south-south-east to Gjeiten and the entrance to Korsfjord, where the main fjord again turned so that the course up to Trondheim where it widened was again north of east. The charioteers had remained concealed all day, resting as best they could, and as daylight faded they prepared for the night's attack as they altered course off Korsfjord. The weather was fine but for a stiff easterly breeze and the lights of Trondheim were readily visible.

There remained about 15 miles to go to the slipping position before the final approach by chariots. Craig and Evens completed their preliminary dressing and Brewster and Brown [the four operators] began as Trondheim came abeam to starboard. The east wind increased steadily and *Arthur* began to pitch into the steep sea set up in the fjord. There was nothing to do but press on at reduced speed in the hope that the sudden storm would blow itself out before they reached the entrance to Asenfjord where *Tirpitz* was berthed. Their luck was out. The chariots could be heard bumping erratically against *Arthur*'s keel and just after 2200 they heard a "loud, grinding, tearing noise" and then a jerk and a shudder as something hit *Arthur*'s propeller. One of the chariots had broken adrift.

Larsen eased *Arthur* into sheltered water and Brewster ordered Evans, who was fully dressed, to go over the side and inspect the remaining chariot. It too was gone. Both chariots had broken adrift and were lost, the towing lugs torn from them and still shackled to the wires secured to *Arthur's* keel. They had come undetected within ten miles of their target and their disappointment was intense.

Maybe the Italian nickname was more apt after all.

The mission was now impossible. The operators and the small crew ended up scuttling *Arthur* and making for shore. All but one of the ten Norwegian and British men made it to the Swedish border. The exception was shot and then captured by the Germans. They put him in the hospital and once he was recuperated, they shot him again, this time as a spy. Thus failed a most innovative attempt to damage *Tirpitz*.

Crewmen on board the battleship, moored in a Norwegian fjord. One of the ship's 38-cm gun turrets is trained abeam, and several camouflage floats are in the distance. (NHHC)

The Germans properly regarded Operation Rainbow as a major failure. At first the British thought the same, but at a Chiefs of Staff meeting held on 14 January 1943 Admiral Pound suggested that the withdrawal of *Hipper* and *Lützow* indicated the Germans were following a policy of preventing their ships from receiving any damage and that this might result from a desire to keep them ready for an Atlantic breakout. Thus, the British remained fixated by a strategy that Raeder had unsuccessfully championed and Hitler had rejected. In fact, at this meeting Pound identified the greatest concern of the Home Fleet as being to prevent a breakout into the Atlantic of German naval forces.

Tirpitz remained in Trondheimfjord during the winter of 1942/43 engaged in an extensive do-it-yourself refit, as there was no dry-dock in Norway that could accommodate her. Repair ships and specialists from Germany helped in the task. The crew even constructed a caisson so they could change the rudder while still afloat. *Tirpitz* was ready for sea trials by 28 December, and she conducted firing trials in January. She returned to full operational status on 24 January and commenced exercises in the Trondheim area. This involved frequently shifting her berth to various anchorages in the large fjord.

Operation Rainbow

ADAPTED FROM "GERMAN ATTACKS ON THE MURMANSK RUN," BY A. E. SOKOL, U.S. NAVAL INSTITUTE *PROCEEDINGS*, DECEMBER 1952

With weather conditions again favoring the defense, a new series of convoys to North Russia was started on December 15, 1942. They were now dispatched in two sections separated by a week. The first section, JW 51 A, of sixteen ships, had an uneventful and safe voyage. The second section, JW 51 B, of fifteen merchant vessels, which left Scotland on December 22, was not quite as lucky and ran into a German task force consisting of the heavy cruisers *Hipper* and *Lützow* and six destroyers.

The attack occurred during a heavy snow storm which greatly reduced visibility. This, together with the gallant defense put up by the four British escorting destroyers and a series of mistakes by the Germans who mistook each other for the enemy and vice versa, kept the German force from reaching the convoy. When after a fight of several hours the British cruisers of the covering force appeared on the scene, the German admiral, assuming them to be

Tirpitz' superstructure showing her main and forward gunnery-control positions. Atop the main position is a radar office housing the FuMo radar. (*Naval Gunnery*)

the vanguard of the British Home Fleet, broke off the engagement and retired in accordance with his orders. The convoy escaped without the loss of a single merchant ship. While two of the British destroyers were sunk, the vastly superior Germans had also lost two of their rapidly-vanishing flotilla units. Operation "Rainbow" thus again ended without success for the German surface ships. But the consequences of this action for the German Navy were even more serious and far-reaching than the escape of an Allied convoy.

Owing to a failure of communications Hitler had first been told that the operation had apparently been a complete success. When the truth was finally learned, he fell into a rage in which he accused the German High Seas Fleet of cowardice and incompetence and blamed it for never fighting actions through to a finish—although he himself had insisted that no undue risks should be taken by the few capital ships. He demanded that all major German warships be scrapped and their guns mounted on land for coastal defense. In this he was eagerly supported by the Commander-in-Chief of the

Luftwaffe, Goering, who pointed out that the maintenance of the heavy ships was tying down squadrons of planes which could be used to better advantage elsewhere and that, anyway, his Air Force could do everything that the warships could. Besides, the steel that would become available through the scrapping of the large vessels could alleviate the general steel shortage of the Germans.

In a memorandum to Hitler, *Großadmiral* Raeder tried to dissuade the Fuehrer from putting his order into effect. He argued that the decommissioning of the heavy German ships would constitute a "victory gained by our enemies without any effort on their part. It will be viewed as a sign of weakness and a lack of understanding of the supreme importance of naval warfare in the approaching final stage of the war." When his reasoning failed to change Hitler's "irrevocable" decision, the admiral—who had always advocated a balanced German fleet including battleships, aircraft carriers, and a separate naval air arm—had no choice but to resign. The Fuehrer appointed Admiral Doenitz, hitherto Admiral of Submarines, to succeed Raeder as Commander-in-Chief of the German Navy.

All hands on deck: a ceremonial occasion in Fættenfjord in 1942. (Aldo Fraccaroli collection, USMM)

A line of destroyers under way. (U.S. Naval Institute photo archive)

As the work was under way Dönitz quickly talked Hitler out of the worse consequences of his order to scrap the fleet's major warships. He and Hitler met on 26 February, and the new chief of staff even obtained permission to send *Scharnhorst*, finally repaired and fully operational, north to join *Tirpitz* in a powerful new strike force. *Tirpitz*, having weathered that storm, was ready for action once again by March, and with a new captain. On 24 February 1943 *Kapitän zur See* Hans Meyer, former captain of the light cruiser *Köln*, relieved Karl Topp, who had been promoted to rear admiral in January and now returned to Germany to

The oiler *Ditchmarschen* was a supply ship purpose-built by the German navy to support its oceanic war on commerce. It was based in Altafjord and served as the main fuel repository for the fleet. One German destroyer man recalled that the ships would fuel before a sortie and then upon their return discharge their oil into the ship, retaining only 5 to 10 percent of capacity in their bunkers. Under these conditions, *Ditchmarschen* would have been a more suitable target than *Tirpitz*, if the objective had been to incapacitate the entire fleet. (U.S. Naval Institute photo archive)

serve as chairman of a commission on shipbuilding.

During these months, even though she was within range of long-range bombers, the RAF made no attacks against *Tirpitz*. There were only 14 fighters in the area at the beginning of December so, notwithstanding the vagaries of the winter weather, it seems an opportunity was missed.

On 11/12 March *Tirpitz*, escorted by the 6th Destroyer Flotilla, left Trondheim for Narvik. In Bogen Bay she joined *Scharnhorst* and *Lützow*. The next day *Vizeadmiral* Kummetz assumed command of the task force, with *Tirpitz* as flagship. On the 23rd, in Operation Silesia, the flotilla transferred to Altafjord, arriving the next day. Supporting the three capital ships were six destroyers—*Steinbrinck*, *Galster*, *Jacobi*, *Riedel*, *Z28*, and *Z29*—along with the torpedo boats *T20* and *T21*. The surface threat to the Murmansk convoys was greater than ever. In fact, it was great enough to cause the Allies to suspend all convoys, using instead the Persian route for most supplies. The political consequences of this decision (on top of the news that there would be no second front in 1943, only a landing on the Mediterranean island of Sicily) caused serious tension in the always delicate alliance between the Soviet Union and the Western democracies. Moreover, there is strong evidence that the Germans and Soviets were discussing a separate peace at this time. Had such a peace come to fruition, *Tirpitz* would have played a role in making it happen.

This powerful German fleet in Altafjord was blockading Murmansk by its very presence. There it spent a quiet summer training and exercising. The British had concentrated six battleships and two fleet carriers in the Mediterranean for the invasion of Sicily. The American fast battleships *Alabama* and

Tirpitz passed through Narvik several times, but Trondheim and Altafjord were her main haunts. This photo of a German boat approaching a dock at Narvik in 1942 shows the dramatic nature of the landscape. The access road winding up the mountainside is particularly striking. (NHHC)

South Dakota stood by in Scapa Flow, but they were needed in the Pacific. The Allies still lacked enough force to be strong everywhere, and during the first half of 1943 the German fleet in being controlled the Barents Sea.

After trials run in early July, Captain Meyer found that the battleship's speed was three knots less than expected. The SKL diary identified the reasons as increased draft, foul bottom, and minor engine defects. "These consequences of prolonged [lack of] docking are probably unavoidable." Staff concluded that a dockyard period in Germany was imperative. It could be deferred to spring 1944 but the coming winter was

their recommended time to do the work. By August naval staff was determined to bring *Tirpitz* south during the new moon in the third week of October 1943. In the meanwhile, in mid-August, planning began for a new operation. This called for *Tirpitz*, *Scharnhorst*, and "at least 10 destroyers" to eliminate what the SKL War Diary described as the "enemy base" on Spitzbergen. Some of the destroyers would carry 75 troops. The targets were the Barentsburg radio station and the airbase and radio station at Langyeardbyen (these were the island's only two settlements), both overlooking Isfjorden (Ice Fjord). "Group North/Fleet welcomed the plan for this additional operation (codeword 'Sizilien') by the Task Force especially on psychological grounds but pointed out the difficulties in regard to oil . . . as well as the risk involved if the enemy with superior forces and aircraft carriers, should accept the challenge to battle without our reconnaissance being able to guarantee the Task Force against surprise."

The navy managed to secure the Führer's permission for this operation and by early September was waiting for the right weather. On 6 September the task force sailed. It consisted of *Tirpitz* and *Scharnhorst* and three destroyer flotillas: the 4th (Z29, Z31, and Z33); the

The ice-capped peaks of Spitzbergen surrounding the waters of Lowe Sound. The site of the raided settlement is on the barren hillside at right. Photographed in July 1942 from the U.S. merchant vessel *Troubadour* during the PQ 17 action. (NHHC)

Tirpitz anchored in Altafjord, bathed in the Northern Lights. She is protected by antitorpedo nets. (NHHC)

5th (Z27, Z30, and *Steinbrinck*); and the 6th (*Galster, Lody,* and *Riedel*). The ships of the 4th and 5th each carried approximately 75 men of the 349th Grenadier Regiment. The plan called for the 4th Flotilla's troops, designated Force Grün, to land at Barentsberg. *Tirpitz,* screened by *Galster* and *Riedel,* would support them while Force *Rot,* embarked in the 5th Division and supported by *Scharnhorst* and *Lody,* would take care of the targets at Longyearbyen. The weather was fair, with good visibility.

The Germans raised the island just after midnight on the 8th and proceeded up Isfjorden. The radio/weather reporting station at Barentsberg broadcast an alarm at 0145 and then went off the air. Barentsberg was defended by a pair of 3-inch guns. These opened fire in defense of the position and were enough of a nuisance that Z29 asked *Tirpitz* for support. *Tirpitz* and her attendant destroyers opened fire, and the shore battery wisely shut up. Meanwhile, *Scharnhorst* proceeded up the fjord to Longyearbyen. The troops started landing at 0430, a half-hour ahead of schedule, and over the course of several hours they destroyed the coal mines at Barentsberg, the radio station, and all other targets as most of the Norwegian defenders

A dramatic image of *Tirpitz* leading *Admiral Scheer* on a sortie. The occasion has been variously identified. (*Signal Magazine,* Enrico Cernuschi)

Barentsberg under fire.
(Rohwer, *War at Sea*)

fled inland. *Tirpitz* fired 52 38-cm and 82 15-cm rounds. This was the only time she used her guns against a surface target. She received 13 of the 74 prisoners taken by the Germans. The Norwegians also lost 11 men killed. Shore batteries lightly damaged three destroyers; the Germans suffered nine deaths and 49 wounded. The force started to reembark troops at 0900 and was under way for home by 1100. On the way it was sighted by the new submarine *Tantalus* on a workup cruise, but she was unable to attack. *Tirpitz* dropped anchor in Altafjord at 1730 on the 9th.

The British had no advance intelligence of this operation. On the 7th aerial reconnaissance reported that *Tirpitz* was not at her anchorage. The Home Fleet sortied that day to be ready in case the Germans were contemplating a breakout into the Atlantic. On the 10th aircraft overflew the island and reported that its facilities and buildings were all destroyed. USS *Tuscaloosa*, escorted by four British destroyers, mounted a relief expedition, arriving on 19 October with 48 personnel and 125 tons of supplies. She also evacuated some of the survivors. The American cruiser's log book remarked on the fact that her mission was probably the farthest north any U.S. Navy vessel had ventured.

The German naval staff expressed their satisfaction with the operation in the SKL War Diary on 9 September:

The operation developed just as Naval Staff had foreseen. What is of importance is not the relatively small strategic success gained but the fact that our heavy units could at long last be put into action again. This has not only had an excellent effect on the morale of the crews, but it has more especially reminded friend and foe alike of the strategic importance which the presence of these naval units far north represents when related to the war situation in general. Furthermore, it was hoped that they would make the enemy feel uneasy. That they also achieved this has been confirmed by the appearance of the enemy forces sighted by our air reconnaissance.

In fact, *Tirpitz* had had no business shooting up a radio station. The raid's military consequences were trivial, and a pair of destroyers could have accomplished the task just as easily. But the human element of war is important, and the Germans recognized that they needed to use their big ships. Their problem was that it was impossible to find suitable uses that carried no risk: in their difficult dance between requirements and restrictions, they had to resort to operations like the Spitzbergen raid.

THE X-CRAFT ATTACK
SEPTEMBER 1943

The crew of *Tirpitz* did not long enjoy the fillip to their morale that destroying the settlements on desolate Spitsbergen had brought.

The crew of *Tirpitz* in dress uniforms gathered aft for a special occasion. The torpedo net and the tarps draped over the main turrets stand out in this image. (*Signal Magazine*, Enrico Cernuschi)

Tirpitz Tale

ADAPTED FROM "*TIRPITZ* TALE," BY BURKE WILKINSON, U.S. NAVAL INSTITUTE *PROCEEDINGS*, APRIL 1954

The attack on the German battleship *Tirpitz* by British X-craft in September, 1943, was one of the most daring feats of the war. *Tirpitz delenda est* [is to be destroyed], the Admiralty decreed. But how? Her favorite hideout at [Altafjord], 200 miles inside the Arctic Circle, seemed the most secure haven in Europe. The fjord bites deeply into the rocky spine of Scandinavia. Sheer cliffs slide into the icy waters.

the battleship's lair, and sowed minefields to seaward. They set patrol craft nosing back and forth along the fixed defenses. They lined the shore with flak batteries. Combined with *Tirpitz's* own firepower, these could put a roof of splintering steel over the hideaway. As a final precaution they draped a triple cordon of anti-torpedo (A/T) nets about the battleship herself. *Tirpitz* was safe, the Nazi Admirals

submersible trimmed down to the vital gear for submerging, surfacing, and delivering a lethal attack within limited range. She was 48 feet long, with a pressure hull just under six feet in diameter. She was fitted with both diesels for surface use and an electric motor for submerged running. Besides the captain, the crew consisted of a sublieutenant Second Officer, a leading seaman who doubled as diver,

Aerial view of Kåfjord looking roughly west to east. (U.S. Naval Institute photo archive)

They effectively screened *Tirpitz* from torpedo-plane attack, made bombing extremely difficult. Sometimes for days these inland arms of the sea are swathed in white mist. It was as if *Tirpitz* had been packed in cotton wool and labeled "do not disturb."

Leaving nothing to chance, the Germans slung anti-submarine (A/S) nets across the entrance to

assured their ex-corporal chief.

But the Royal Navy had other ideas. Rear Admiral C. B. Barry (Admiral, Submarines) sums them up in his official report: The X type of small submarine was evolved as a result of the problem of how enemy main units could be attacked in their heavily defended and inaccessible fleet anchorages. The X-craft was a

and a coxswain with the rating of engine room artificer. The explosive charges were carried outboard in cases attached to the main hull.

By May 1942 successful trials had been completed and a contract placed with Messrs. Vickers Armstrong Ltd. for the construction of six X-craft. These were delivered in the first two weeks of January, 1943.

At the same time, volunteers were requested "for special and hazardous service." Among the volunteers was Lt. Donald Cameron, R.N.R., a 27-year-old reservist who had served in the Merchant Navy since the age of 16. Also reporting in was Lt. Godfrey Place, R.N., a 23-year-old submariner and holder of the Distinguished Service Cross.

The location selected for training was as lonely as could be. "Port HHZ" was located at Loch Cairnbawn, one of those sea lochs in the far northwest of Scotland where special security measures could be maintained. Operation Source was classified Most Secret and, thanks to the mists and the moors and the vigilance of the security officers, it remained so.

There Cameron and Place were joined by Lieutenant H. Henty-Creer, R.N.V.R., and a small group of men picked for their physical fitness and proved courage. Their headquarters was a manor house near the loch. Living conditions simulated the small submarines they were to man. Sleeping quarters were cramped. Rations consisted in large part of concentrated food. The manor house itself was made even damper than usual.

From July until the commencement of the operation full scale exercises and attacks against capital ships were carried out. This period was also devoted to perfecting the towing of X-craft by submarines.

Here, in the Barry report, was the explanation of one of the mysteries which had surrounded the mission. How had the small submarines with a range of only 200 miles negotiated 1,100 miles of open sea before the final run-in to the target area? There had been many rumors—mystery ships, secret Norwegian bases and the like—now the truth was out: with

The brass inspects an X-craft. Rear Admiral G. B. Barry (Admiral Submarines) gingerly lowering himself down the hatch of a midget submarine while the First Lord of the Admiralty (on the dock) looks on. (U.S. Naval Institute photo archive)

"passage" crews on board, the X-craft were towed by full-sized submarines. Arrived off Altafjord, the fresh "operational" crews took over, having made the long journey on board the towing submarines.

It had originally been hoped that the raid could be made in the spring of 1943, before the hours of darkness shortened. March 9 was considered the latest possible date. But neither crews nor craft were ready. Reluctantly Admiral Barry informed the Vice Chief of the Naval Staff that the operation would have to be postponed.

This wise decision was typical of the Navy's thorough approach to the whole operation. The time gained proved invaluable; it ensured that both the crews and the craft were trained and perfected to that concert pitch so vital to such an operation, Barry noted. The postponement paid off.

Cameron, Place, Henty-Creer and the rest spent a busy summer in their remote corner of Scotland. Thanks to the Commander-in-Chief, Home Fleet, who made capital ships available, and to the Boom Defence Department, who draped steel nets

X-craft coming into dock after a day of training.
(U.S. Naval Institute photo archive)

around the ships, they had live targets to practice on. And in the evenings they studied charts and contour maps of the lair of *Tirpitz* until they knew it like the kitchen garden of the manor house: first came the mined area in the open sea, athwart Soroy Sund; then the narrow 15-mile funnel of Stjern Sund. Once through the funnel they would be in Altafjord. At the inmost end of Altafjord was an almost landlocked little bay called Kåfjord. Across the 1,000-yard entrance to Kåfjord was the double line of A/S nets, well patrolled. Nearly three miles behind the nets, moored by the stern to bollards ashore and with two bow anchors clawing at the rocky bottom 120 feet below, *Tirpitz* was wont to take her ease.

Typical of the thoroughness of Operation Source was the method employed to assure accurate Photo Reconnaissance (PR). Altafjord was of course well out of range of home-based PR aircraft. In late August of 1943 a British destroyer made the Murmansk run with a PR crew on board. Spitfires to fly the crew were based in North Russia, and Catalinas were laid on for a shuttle service from North Russia with the actual photographs.

In early September the highwayman was on the loose. *Tirpitz* slipped her anchor chains, dashed the 400 miles to Spitzbergen on a "daring attack" against the coal mines and the small garrison there, and raced back to her hiding place again.

The date set for the attack—"Day D"—was September 20.

On September 10 Admiral Barry arrived at Port HHZ to wish the crews Godspeed. "Any doubts," he later observed, "which I might have entertained could not possibly survive the infectious confidence of these young men. This confidence was not the outcome of youthful daredevilry, but was based on a firm conviction that their submarines were capable of doing all their crews demanded. . . ."

At well-spaced intervals, the six submarines—*Truculent, Syrtis, Stubborn, Thrasher, Seanymph* [sic] and *Sceptre*—slipped down the loch.

The passage was uneventful from the 11th to 14th September. Good weather was experienced and all submarines made good speed with their X-craft dived in tow.

In the meantime some electrifying news had come from Russia by Catalina. Latest PR sorties showed that the Altafjord area was full of big game. The pocket battleship *Lützow* had dropped her hook in Lange Fjord, one of those finger-like bays openings off Altafjord. Just inside the

Tirpitz at Kåfjord showing the antitorpedo net and the causeway to shore. The B and D turrets are darkened, and the other two highlighted to make her appear to be a two-turret ship from the air. (*Warship*)

parted her tow. She did not again make contact with *Seanymph* (which immediately turned back in search) until the next day. Later X.8 developed a leak in the buoyancy chamber of her starboard charge. Trim became difficult to maintain. One charge, then the second had to be jettisoned. Finally, almost out of control, X.8 was sunk as a liability, to the bitter disappointment of Lt. McFarlane and his crew. *Lützow* would have to wait.

Loss of X.8 was a blow, but the fate of X.9 was far sadder. Somewhere in the small hours of the 16th, while in tow submerged, she broke loose. It was not until the time for her next breathing spell at 0920 that the tow was hauled in and found to have parted. No trace of Passage Commanding Officer Sublieutenant E. Kearon, R.N.V.R., and his crew has ever been found.

September 17 (D-3) was the day set for the transfer of the operational crews to the X-craft. But the weather was deteriorating rapidly. By evening the wind was Force 4 with a 4–5 Sea. The change-over was postponed. The next day the sea had leveled off, the wind was a breeze and visibility good. The submarines were able to make accurate fixes. After dark, *Thrasher*, *Truculent*, *Stubborn*, and *Sceptre*, lying some 15 miles off the gaunt Norwegian headlands, slipped their X-craft. For the rest of the operation they were to stand by as pickets, on the alert to attack anything their precocious spawn might flush.

Now the first team took over. The three X-craft whose objective was *Tirpitz* were to proceed at will. But their intentions were the same: to run surfaced across the mined area to the westward of Soroy during the night of September 20, then to work

entrance to Kåfjord the battle cruiser *Scharnhorst* lay at anchor. And *Tirpitz* herself was in her playpen at the landward end.

This information was signaled to the submarines at sea and Target Plan Number 4 ordered. This allocated X.5 (Lt. H. Henty-Creer), X.6 (Lt. D. Cameron), and X.7 (Lt.

B. C. G. Place) to attack *Tirpitz*. X.9 (Lt. T. L. Martin) and X.10 (Lt. K. R. Hudspeth) were assigned to *Scharnhorst* and X.8 (Lt. B. M. McFarlane) to *Lützow*.

That was on 15 September (D-5). Already occupational difficulties were setting in. X.8, while dived in tow of *Seanymph* at eight knots, their way up Stjern Sund, submerged, during the daylight hours of the 21st, reaching Altafjord by dusk. The second night was to be spent recharging batteries in the vicinity of the Brattholm Islands, four miles from Kåfjord itself. By daylight each craft intended to be at the entrance to the Fjord. To preserve the element of surprise no X-craft was to attack before 0100Z on the 22nd. Charges were to be set for approximately 0830Z, in order to give the craft time to withdraw.

Let us first follow the fortunes of Cameron and his X.6.

Somewhere during the passage up Stjern Sund a defect in the periscope developed. X.6 managed to reach the recharging area and spent a disturbed night recharging

ALTAFJORD AND THE X-CRAFT ATTACK

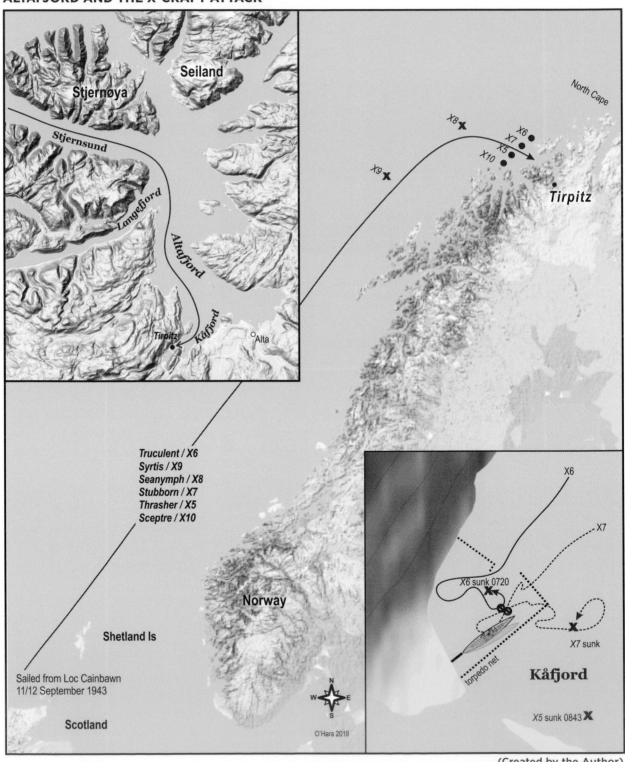

Seiland

Stjernøya

Stjernsund

Langefjord

Altafjord

Tirpitz   Kåfjord   ○ Alta

North Cape

X8 ✖
X9 ✖
X6 ●
X7 ●
X5 ●
X10 ●

Tirpitz

Truculent / X6
Syrtis / X9
Seanymph / X8
Stubborn / X7
Thrasher / X5
Sceptre / X10

Norway

Shetland Is

Sailed from Loc Cainbawn
11/12 September 1943

Scotland

N
W ✦ E
S

O'Hara 2019

X6

X7

X6 sunk 0720 ✖

torpedo net

X7 sunk ✖

Kåfjord

X5 sunk 0843 ✖

(Created by the Author)

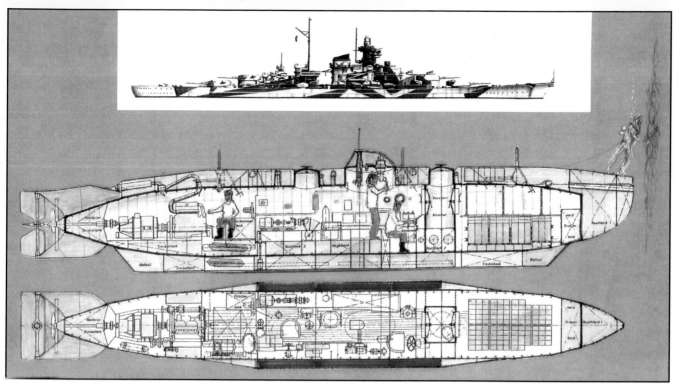

Drawing of the internal arrangements of the British X-craft. (F. Harrauer, Enrico Cernuschi)

and trying to strip and clear the flooded 'scope.

Just before two in the morning she left the lee of the Brattholms to try her luck against the defenses of Kåfjord. Dodging a small ferry boat and a patrol vessel, she slipped through a gap in the A/S boom at 0505. But the 'scope clouded over again. Cameron went to 60 feet to strip and clean it.

Coming to periscope depth Cameron found X.6 was running so close to the moored tanker *Nordmark* that he had to alter course to avoid hitting her mooring buoy. By 0705 he had by a combination of dead reckoning and an occasional look-see, closed the shore side of the net defense around *Tirpitz*.

Meanwhile life in Kåfjord pursued its usual course. At 0500, hands were called, normal A/A defense and anti-sabotage watches ashore and afloat were set, the gates in the A/T nets were opened for boat traffic, and the

hydrophone listening office ceased work.

Now Cameron slipped through the small boat gap in the torpedo net. Nothing lay between him and *Tirpitz* but a short expanse of open water. Suddenly, sickeningly, X.6 ran aground in shoal water on the north shore of the enclosure, within 200 yards of her objective. She broke surface momentarily. Lookouts on board the battleship sighted her and took her for a porpoise.

Backing frantically to get clear of the ground, she broke surface again five minutes later, about 80 yards abeam of *Tirpitz*. Again she was sighted and this time identified for what she was.

Cameron's 'scope was flooded again, his gyro compass put out of action by the grounding and the violent angles the boat had then assumed. He steered blindly in the general direction of the target, fouled something hanging from the far (starboard) side of *Tirpitz*,

shook himself clear and surfaced to find himself close on the port bow of the battleship. A brisk fire from small arms greeted him. Fortunately he was too close to the ship for any of the heavy A/A or the main guns to bear.

The Barry report sums up the closing minutes of the strenuous life of the X.6 as succinctly as could be: "Realizing that escape was hopeless, Cameron destroyed the most secret equipment, backed his craft down until his stern was scraping *Tirpitz'* hull abreast 'B' turret, released his charges and scuttled the craft." X.6 started to sink as a power boat from *Tirpitz* came alongside, picked off the crew of four and vainly attempted to take X.6 in tow, but X.6 followed her explosives to the bottom.

Tirpitz first sighted X.6 at 0707. By 0730 Cameron and crew were prisoners on board her, and his two tremendous charges lay under her belly, set to explode in less than an hour's time.

Now the alarm was fully raised. Destroyers were getting up steam, smaller craft tad-poling nervously about. After the first confusion *Tirpitz* took reasonable precautions: action stations were sounded, water-tight doors closed, and divers sent down for full inspection. At 0736 the order was given to prepare for sea.

At 0740 came the first clue that more than one enemy craft was attacking. X.7 was spotted, dead ahead, just outside the A/T net. Then she was gone again.

Had she carried out her attack? Were there other craft lurking in the fjord? Captain Meyer of the *Tirpitz* had a grave decision. Should he head for open water and the unknown hazards which that entailed? Or should he shift his position inside the enclosure? Meyer chose the latter course. First he ordered the small-boat gates in the A/T nets shut, then he heaved in on the starboard anchor cable and veered the port cable. This moved the shackled ship as far away as possible from the position where Cameron had sunk the X.6.

But the skipper reckoned without Place and the X.7.

After X.7 was turned loose by *Stubborn*, she made a surfaced run through the minefields off Soroy. Diving in the early hours of 21 September, she reached her recharging position off the Brattholms toward evening and spent the night there. At 0045 she started on her great adventure into Kåfjord.

By 0400 X.7 was through the gap in the A/S defenses, diving deep to avoid a minelayer outward bound. This temporary blindness brought trouble, for later she fouled the square of torpedo nets behind which *Lützow* had lain, now vacant. Place worked his craft free, but it took an hour. By

0600 he was clear at last and heading for the target at periscope depth.

Place had less luck than Cameron during his run-in. He decided to pass under the close protection A/T nets, figuring that 75 feet down would give him a good margin of clearance. But the Germans had rigged their nets surface-to-bottom, making them do double duty as A/S nets. X.7 enmeshed herself in the closely-woven grommets. Place blew to full buoyancy and surfaced, going astern to the northward. Almost immediately he submerged, unspotted, and was foul of the net again. Another five minutes of backing and filling and he was clear, coming gently to the surface. Here is Place's own account of the final phase: "By some extraordinary lucky chance we must have either passed under the nets or worked our way through the boat passage, for on breaking surface *Tirpitz*, with no intervening nets, was sighted right ahead not more than 30 yards away. Forty feet was ordered and X.7 at full speed struck *Tirpitz* at twenty feet on the port side and slid gently under the keel, where the starboard charge was released in the full shadow of the ship. Going slowly astern the port charge was released about 150 to 200 feet further aft."

The time was approximately 0722. And it was high time to get out, with Cameron's charges and his own set to go off within the hour, and maybe Henty-Creer's too. Godfrey Place got. But his compass had gone wild by now and he had limited ideas on where he was. At 60 feet down he was back in the net again, with only 1,200-lb. left in his third and last air bottle.

In the next 45 minutes X.7 was in and out of a lot of nets. While at 40 feet she suddenly shook free while still going ahead. Porpoise-like she slithered over the top of the nets on

the surface. The time was 0740. Now *Tirpitz* spotted her at last and knew there was more than one foe at large in her lair. *Tirpitz* opened fire with all that could be brought to bear, which was fortunately only machine guns. A hail of bullets hit the casing. Place immediately vented all main ballast tanks and plummeted to 120 feet. In trying to put as much water as possible between himself and the coming explosion he hit another net.

The time was 0812. A tremendous explosion shook the X.7 from stem to stern. It also shook her out of the net. Place surfaced. "It was tiresome," said he, "to see *Tirpitz* still afloat." He wondered if the explosion had been one of his own well-laid charges or a depth charge indicating counter-attack. He took X.7 to the bottom to think things over. Compasses and diving gauges were by now out of action but structural damage was surprisingly slight. Yet X.7 was out of control and kept breaking surface and getting herself shot at. Random depth-charging was going on too. Place decided to abandon ship. He surfaced accordingly. First out the hatch—the post of danger—he found himself close by a moored target and was able to step on to it.

X.7 was in the final throes. At 0835, before any of the others could escape, she sank. By use of Davis Submarine Escape Apparatus Sublieutenant Aitken, the Second Officer, was able to surface three hours later. No trace of the two remaining members of the crew was ever found.

Both Place and Aitken were taken aboard *Tirpitz*, just as Cameron and his crew had been.

The rest of the story is quickly told. *Tirpitz'* log reported two heavy consecutive detonations to port, 1/10 of a second apart, at 0812. It seems

Reconnaissance photo of *Tirpitz* probably taken by a Mosquito popping over the top of the hill, showing how steep the drop to the ship's decks was. (U.S. Naval Institute photo archive)

likely that all four charges laid by the two X-craft detonated at this time. *Tirpitz* heaved five or six feet out of the water before settling back, listing to port. The explosion extended from amidships to aft. On the port side, a tremendous column of water leapt skyward. Casualties, mostly to engine room personnel, were one killed, [about] 40 wounded.

Only the action of the captain in moving the bows to starboard on her cables had saved her from complete destruction. As it was, the damage was impressive. By 0942 there were 500 tons of water in the ship, mostly in the middle and port turbine rooms. All three main engines were put out of action. Nearly all the lighting and electrical equipment was out.

Before the explosion, Cameron and his crew had been well treated on board the German battleship. They were drinking coffee and schnapps when the charges went off. Lights went out, doors jammed, fire extinguishers fell off the bulkheads and started to belch foam. Captain Meyer, "foaming like one of his own extinguishers," ordered all four prisoners shot as saboteurs, then changed his mind.

Shortly after the explosion, a third X-craft, undoubtedly Henty-Creer's X.5, was sighted some 500 yards outside the torpedo nets. *Tirpitz* opened fire, and she sank. Patrol craft circled the oil slick, dropping depth charges. The rest is silence, and a salute to Henty-Creer, of whose equal valor there can be no doubt.

As for X.10, she was in trouble with her trim from almost the very start. Then the periscope-raising motor caught fire, so that 'scope was forced to remain in a fully-raised position. With the utmost reluctance Lt. Hudspeth decided to abandon the attack, a decision later fully endorsed by Admiral Barry. For no less than eight days she stayed in the area, seeking her mother submarine. On 28 September contact was finally made with *Stubborn* off Soroy.

Eight days after the attack, the Germans salvaged Godfrey Place's X.7 from a position 400 yards off the bow of the crippled battleship and outside the torpedo nets. The whole of her bow was missing. Not even a deck bolt of the X.6 was ever found.

So *Tirpitz* was left alone in the fjord, 1,500 miles from the nearest major repair base. The lair had boomeranged into a trap. *Scharnhorst* and other German fleet units fled to safer hiding.

On 24 September Dönitz reported to Hitler that the damage inflicted on *Tirpitz* in the X-craft raid was as follows:

(1.) Control stations for heavy anti-aircraft guide partly out of order, but repairs with the resources available on board will be attempted.

(2.) Several range-finders are out of order. Repairs with the resources available on board are only partly possible.

(3.) Engine and Power Plant: All the power stations are out of action for the present because the bolts in the bed plates have been torn out. A definite statement as to when the power turbines will be in service again will probably be available in a week's time. It is expected that it will be possible to put the central and starboard power turbines back into action.

(4.) The double bottom has been damaged and leaks have sprung in the inner one. Intake of water to the extent of 800 cubic meters (power station 2 flooded) has so far been reduced to 300 cubic meters by pumping. The power station is still out of action.

(5.) Casualties: One killed, 37 injured.

Actually, this estimation proved optimistic. An assessment made four days later acknowledged that all three main engines were nonfunctional, Generator Room No. 2 was disabled, some of the main turbines had damage to their blades, no. 2 rudder was nonfunctional, and six shaft-bearing covers were broken.

Dönitz and Hitler agreed that regardless of the damage and the complete lack of facilities in Altafjord, it was important to make the ship operational and that the work would have to be done in situ. It was just too risky to try to tow her to Germany, and even once there she would only attract an ever-increasing scale of air attack. Thus, work was begun using personnel from the repair ship *Neumark*. Skilled workmen and technicians were brought up from Germany and housed in the accommodation ship *New York*, a former liner. The critical task was to repair the propulsion plant and get the battleship fit for sea. All the major machinery foundations were cracked, many turbine rotors were distorted, and there were cracks and breaks in valves and in the coupling flanges of the shafting. It proved especially challenging to realign the shafts, as the repairs required adjustments as great as 13-

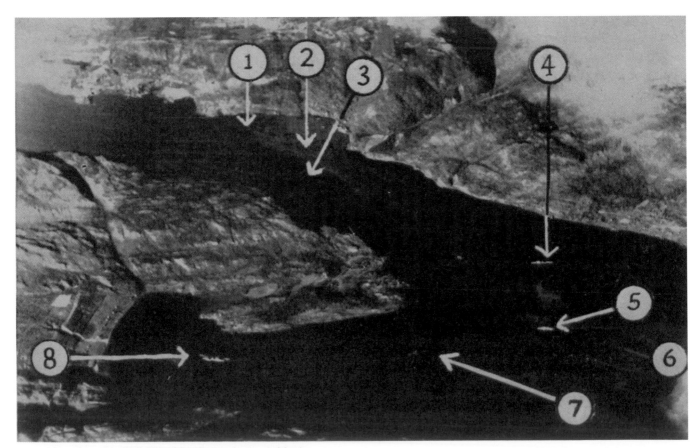

After the raid. (U.S. Naval Institute photo archive)

cm. The explosion had lifted D turret from its roller track, and when all the weight crashed back down the roller bearings had been damaged. This prevented the turret from training, and this damage was irreparable, as there was no crane available to lift such a weight and reposition the turret. The port side no. 3 15-cm turret was also jammed.

The historians and naval engineers Garzke and Dulin write: "These repairs to the *Tirpitz* during 1943–1944, without sufficient shipyard facilities and under severe weather conditions, were one of the most notable feats of naval engineering during the Second World War."

The Germans were able to work throughout the winter without molestation from Allied forces except for one air raid conducted by Soviet IL-4 twin-engine bombers of the 36th Regiment on the night of 11/12 February. Fifteen aircraft armed with 1,000-kg bombs took off, but only four found the target, achieving one near miss that caused minor damage.

By this time the crew and imported workers had replaced the port rudder and overhauled and aligned

Tirpitz in Norwegian waters. (NHHC)

Underwater Explosions

ADAPTED FROM *BATTLESHIPS: AXIS AND NEUTRAL BATTLESHIPS IN WORLD WAR II REV. ED.* BY WILLIAM H. GARZKE JR. AND ROBERT O. DULIN JR., NAVAL INSTITUTE PRESS

The most spectacular damage sustained by the *Tirpitz* was from non-contact explosions. The 2-ton mines laid by the X-craft created explosive forces far in excess of any design loads that had been derived from the *Falk* Experiments. It seems that the second pressure pulse was the most severe and this might be attributed to the explosives' amplification on the seabed. Various sections of the ship were set in motion at different periods of time, since there were two major sources of explosive loadings. The ship, as a whole, was deformed momentarily by the forces of the explosions, causing local oscillations of plates and frames, while larger items such as main bulkheads tended to vibrate. In turn, the whole ship vibrated as a beam with two or more nodes. This phenomenon is termed *whipping*. . . . Whipping threw men about on the decks and caused damage to loose objects and equipment on foundations. The tiedown bolts for equipment on board the *Tirpitz* were not designed to withstand the large oscillations generated by this size of explosion. The *Tirpitz* was the largest warship put out of action in World War II through a shock response to a non-contact explosion.

the propeller shafts. Ultra was providing the Admiralty in London a steady stream of information that supplemented more traditional forms of intelligence. For example, a Soviet photograph taken on 15 February showed *Tirpitz* amid her clustered repair vessels and barges making smoke. On 3 March the battleship's forward turrets fired at a floating target. On 15/16 March the ship ran trials that revealed strong vibrations at high speeds, indicating more work was required. Then the repair ships started departing. It was clear to the Allies that Tirpitz was once again a threat that had to be accounted for. A crew member of Z30 recalled, "It was a moment of great joy to everyone on board the task force at that time to get the *Tirpitz* afloat again, but the joy didn't last long."

The RAF was focused on their strategic bombing campaign and was clearly reluctant to mount a long-range raid against *Tirpitz*. This left it to the navy, and on 29 January 1944 the First Sea Lord, now Admiral Andrew Cunningham, asked the commander of the Home Fleet, now Admiral Bruce Fraser, to prepare a carrier strike against *Tirpitz* sometime in the period of 7–16 March.

OPERATION TUNGSTEN AND CARRIER ATTACKS

APRIL–JUNE 1944

By the beginning of 1944 British carrier aviation had progressed a long way since *Victorious'* March 1942 attack on *Tirpitz*. There were more ships (although not better ships), and there were better aircraft (although performance problems continued to limit results), but as the events of April–August 1944 would prove, the Royal Navy still had far to go before it could deliver an effective attack from a flight deck against a heavily defended battleship.

At the beginning of 1944 there were 43 completed flattops in British service, but only 14 were operational. There were five fleet carriers: *Formidable* and the venerable *Furious* sailed with the Home Fleet, *Illustrious* was in transit to the Indian Ocean along with the transport/repair light carrier *Unicorn*, while *Victorious* was in refit and *Indomitable* was under repair. There were 37 escort carriers, of which five were with convoys in the Atlantic. One was escorting convoys in the Indian Ocean, and four were acting as transports, bringing over American carrier aircraft like the Corsair F4U, the Hellfighter F6F, and the Avenger TBF. Fifteen were in refit or being modified, four were in repair, and eight were American-made vessels just completing and awaiting modification before entering British service. New British types like the Fairey Barracuda and Firefly were flying with the fleet. The last British carrier operations of note

This torpedo/dive-bomber first entered service in July 1943. More than 2,500 were delivered to the FAA and served throughout the remainder of the war. The Fairey Barracuda was a refinement of the British quest to develop an effective multiuse carrier strike aircraft, but it was slow, with an effective speed only 35 knots faster than the biwing Albacore, and had a low ceiling. It was inferior to its more specialized American counterparts like the TBF Avenger and the SBC2 Helldiver, which were 60 mph faster. (Public Domain)

Tirpitz on her initial trials after repairing damage from the September 1943 X-craft raid. This photo was taken on 16 March 1944 from the destroyer *Z30*. (U.S. Naval Institute photo archive)

had been in the Mediterranean in September 1943. It was, to say the least, a hectic time for British naval aviation.

Vice Admiral Henry Moore, second in command of the Home Fleet, supervised the planning and execution of the carrier attack against *Tirpitz*, codenamed "Tungsten." Tungsten was originally intended for mid-March but was delayed two weeks so *Victorious*, just coming out of refit, could work up her new squadrons and participate. The delay allowed the Barracuda squadrons assigned to the attack more time to practice. It also allowed for several more Barracudas to be adapted to carry a new 1,600-lb armor-piercing bomb that was just entering service. This was the only bomb the aircraft could carry that had a chance of penetrating the battleship's armored deck and do real damage. Training wrapped up with a full-scale dress rehearsal of all units involved on 28 March.

Good intelligence was critical to the operation's success. On 28 February a photo-reconnaissance unit arrived in Murmansk. On 26 March the reconnaissance Spitfires scheduled daily flights. However, in the seven days between 27 March and 2 April, the weather was such that the aircraft were only able to fly on three days.

For Operation Tungsten, the British deployed two battleships, two fleet carriers, four escort carriers, four light cruisers, and 15 destroyers. Because of the great variation in speed between the fleet and escort carriers, the ships deployed in two formations.

The Worldwide Implications of *Tirpitz* and the War at Sea

On 17 and 18 February the fast carriers and battleships of the U.S. Third Fleet launched Operation Hailstone, a massive raid on the main Japanese main naval base at Truk in the Caroline Islands. The Japanese Combined Fleet, however, withdrew before the attack and sent a good portion of its strength to Singapore. This redeployment, which intelligence put at two fleet carriers, seven battleships, five heavy cruisers, and two dozen destroyers,

seemed to threaten the British Eastern Fleet (the carrier *Illustrious*, two old but modernized battleships, an old battle cruiser, and assorted cruisers and destroyers), which was no better able to deal with a strong Japanese force than it had been two years before when the Combined Fleet had rampaged through the Indian Ocean. Britain's Eastern Fleet clearly required reinforcement. The two available modern battleships, *Duke of York* and *Anson*, were committed to protecting

the Murmansk convoys against *Tirpitz*. As for the carriers: H. P. Wilmott summaries the situation very well in "Grave of a Dozen Schemes" (U.S. Naval Institute *Proceedings*, 1996):

> Britain's carrier problem was that, with the exception of the *Illustrious*, all of its modern fleet carriers were being refitted or completed in February 1944. With the *Indomitable*, almost lost off Sicily the previous July,

On 30 March Force 1 sailed from Scape Flow. This included:

- Battleships: *Duke of York* (flag of Admiral B. Fraser) and *Anson*

- Fleet aircraft carrier: *Victorious* (24 Barracudas, 21 Corsairs)

- Light cruiser: *Belfast*

- Destroyers: *Onslaught, Javelin, Piorun* (Polish), *Sioux* (Canadian), and *Algonquin* (Canadian)

After conducting exercises, this formation headed to a position east of the Faeroes Islands while the destroyers fueled in the Faeroes and then joined Formation 2. They were replaced by the freshly fueled *Milne, Matchless, Marne, Ursa,* and *Undaunted.* Force 1 then headed northeast to cover the Murmansk convoy JW 58 of 47 merchant ships, which had sailed from Scotland on 27 March.

Force 2 sailed from Scapa Flow at 1900 on the 30th of March. It included:

- Fleet carrier: *Furious* (18 Barracudas, 15 Seafires)

- Escort carriers: *Searcher* (20 Wildcats), *Emperor* (20 Hellcats), *Pursuer* (20 Wildcats), *Fencer* (10 Wildcats, 9 Swordfish)

- Light cruisers: *Royalist* (flag of Vice Admiral H. Moore), *Sheffield,* and *Jamaica*

- Destroyers: *Virago, Verulam, Vigilant, Swift,* and *Wakeful*

- Fleet tankers: *Blue Ranger* and *Brown Ranger*

Force 2 sailed to a position near the Faeroes, where it was joined by the destroyers that had refueled there.

Although *Victorious* was a veteran ship, her aircrews were neophytes; for her two Corsair squadrons and her Barracudas this was their first combat mission. *Furious* was a month out of refit, and her Barracudas had participated in one offensive operation (Bayleaf) against coastal shipping in Norwegian waters, on 24 February. *Emperor* and *Pursuer* were also rookies, having participated in just one Atlantic convoy operation each.

Moore intended to attack *Tirpitz* on the 4th, but at 1435 on the 1 April Fraser received an Enigma decryption that indicated *Tirpitz* would be leaving her anchorage on the 3rd to conduct speed trials; Moore advanced the operation by a day. This required the escort carriers to steam at their full speed of 17 knots for more than 24 hours so they could keep their rendezvous with *Victorious.* The two tankers, escorted by *Javelin* and *Piorun,* proceeded independently to a point 300 miles northwest of Altafjord where they would be available to refuel destroyers at need.

Forces 1 and 2 united at 1620 on the 2nd whereupon Fraser took *Duke of York, Matchless,* and *Marne* and sailed northwest to be in position to intervene on behalf of JW.58 or the carrier force as needed. Vice Admiral Moore took the carriers and steered for the flying off position, arriving at 0415 on the 3rd. According to the report of *Victorious:* "By 0300 on 3rd April it appeared that everything was in our favour. So far as we knew we had not been sighted, and flying conditions were perfect for putting the operation into effect. There was a light offshore wind and visibility was in fact so good

being refitted at Norfolk, the British had taken advantage of the dual neutralization of enemy battle forces in Europe (September 1943 had coincided with the crippling of the *Tirpitz* and the surrender of the Italian fleet) to dock both the *Formidable* and *Victorious.* . . . [T]he Admiralty had intended to have the *Renown, Illustrious,* and *Victorious* with the Eastern Fleet by March 1944 in readiness for the move to the Pacific in mid-year; but

the refits proved more extensive than anticipated and timetables had slipped. By February the Admiralty calculated that the *Victorious* would not be ready to sail until April, the *Formidable* and *Indomitable* not before June. The *Indefatigable* was expected to enter service in late May and would then relieve the *Furious,* and in turn she would be released from service with the Home Fleet when the *Implacable* was commissioned. Thus, in Feb-

ruary 1944 the Admiralty had no fleet carriers in service with which to reinforce the Eastern Fleet and would not be able to do so for several months.

The solution to this conundrum was the temporary assignment of the USS *Saratoga* to the British Eastern Fleet. Thus, *Tirpitz's* operational status, which forced Great Britain to hold forces in home waters, affected the order of battle of even the U.S. Navy's Pacific fast carrier task forces.

HMS *Indomitable*. She was still under repair at the time of Tungsten but participated in the later raids against *Tirpitz*. (NHHC)

OVERVIEW OF OPERATION TUNGSTEN

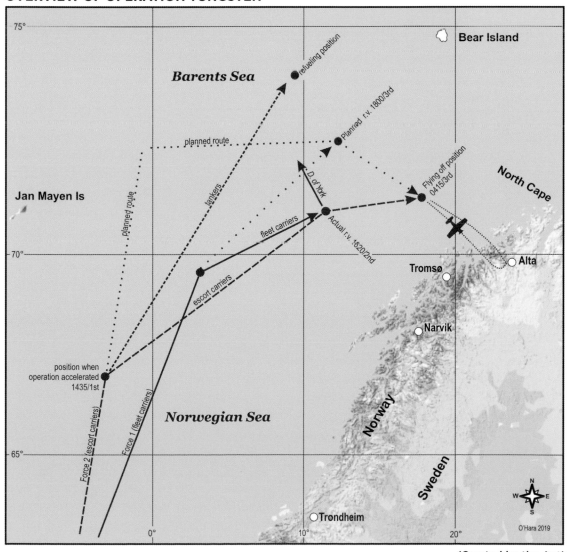

(Created by the Author)

that while landing on the strikes later we sighted the Norwegian coast at a distance of about 50 miles."

Although the weather was good, especially for early spring, the British were operating in one of the world's most challenging maritime environments. The carrier deck crews warmed up engines and swapped hangared aircraft for those parked on deck, giving machines exposed to spray and the elements a chance to be warmed up before participating in the second strike.

The plan of attack called for two strikes taking off an hour apart.

TUNGSTEN STRIKES, 3 APRIL 1944

Strike	Planes	Type	Squadron	Carrier	Lost
First	12	Barracuda	827	*Victorious*	
First	9	Barracuda	830	*Furious*	1 to flak
First	11	Corsairs	1834	*Victorious*	
First	10	Hellcats	800	*Emperor*	
First	10	Wildcats	881	*Pursuer*	
First	10	Wildcats	882	*Searcher*	
Second	11	Barracuda	829	*Victorious*	2*
Second	9	Barracuda	831	*Furious*	
Second	10	Corsairs	1836	*Victorious*	
Second	10	Hellcats	804	*Emperor*	1**
Second	10	Wildcats	896	*Pursuer*	
Second	10	Wildcats	898	*Searcher*	
CAP	18	Seafires	801/880	*Furious*	
CAP	8	Wildcats	?	*Fencer*	
CAP	2	Corsairs	1836	*Victorious*	
A/S	12	Swordfish	842	*Fencer*	

* ONE CRASHED AFTER LAUNCH, ONE TO FLAK.
** DITCHED DUE TO DAMAGE. PILOT RESCUED.
CAP = COMBAT AIR PATROL.

German defenses did not include any fighters (British intelligence thought there were at least four based at Alta). There were 40 fighters at Petasmo and Kirkenes, but they were supporting the army fighting east of Kirkenes. The area's defenses included two antiaircraft cruisers, *Nymphe* and *Thetis*, which carried six 105-mm, six 20-mm, and two 40-mm guns each. Flak units consisted of five batteries of 75-mm to 155-mm guns in the Alta area and several light batteries protecting *Tirpitz* herself.

The first wave started lifting off the flight decks at 0415 (local Z+2), and by 0436 it was formed up and heading for *Tirpitz* at 135 knots, the cruising speed of the Barracudas. The Wildcats flying overhead cover had to weave back and forth to keep station. The aircraft started at low altitude to avoid radar detection and climbed to 10,000 feet when 25 miles from the coast, which they crossed at 0508, 37 miles from their target. German radar picked up the intruders at 0505, but *Tirpitz* did not get word until 0524. According to Captain Meyer's report (times are one hour in advance of British):

on [3 April] sea readiness was ordered for 0530 (slack water). The net enclosure maneuvers started according to plan. The 3 stern cables were cast off and the port anchor weighed at 0635. While the starboard anchor was being weighed it was observed that a smoke screen had been started from on shore. It was also reported . . . that more than 32 aircraft were about 43 miles NW of Kaa Fjord proceeding on course South. The captain consequently ordered the aircraft alarm to be sounded on board. At that time the starboard flak watch were at their stations and the main flak was manned. The ship was battened down for action. . . . At the time the ship was attacked by gunfire, i.e., about 0630. . . . [T]he ship was under way and on her course for leaving harbour. Owing to the short notice the "crash" closing up of watertight doors had only been 80% completed. The A.A. armament was ready to open fire.

The first wave appeared before smoke could cloak the ship. Fighters swooped down to spray the decks with 0.50-caliber bullets. Their job was to ease the way for the dive-bombers by suppressing the ship's antiaircraft guns. From the German perspective, "the aircraft flying

Antiaircraft ship *Nymphe*. This vessel was the ex-Norwegian coastal-defense ship *Tordenskjold* (1897, 3,900 tons). In German service she carried six 10.5-cm, two 40-mm, and 14 20-mm guns. (U.S. Naval Institute photo archive)

to port flew along the ridge of the mountains, making use of every dip, and so low parallel to the ship that they themselves could only see the foretop, thus making it impossible for the lower lying guns and controls to fire at them. When these aircraft were in a position between 220 degrees and 240 degrees from the ship, they suddenly (from a distance of 2,200 yards) 'hedge-hopped' over the mountains and dived on to the ship firing with all their guns." A pilot of 882 Squadron wrote: "We whistled down over forested hills . . . [and] shot across the fjord in a straggling line abreast shooting into the battleship. . . . Various missiles appeared to be whizzing in all directions. . . . Very exciting!" The

fighters zoomed in one after the other, firing on the ship and nearby flak batteries. The Barracudas were right behind them.

The bombers lined up and started to dive on the battleship flying from stern to stem (because studies had shown that more hits were likely attacking lengthwise). They were supposed to drop from above 3,000 feet for optimum bomb penetration, but all came in lower to make hitting easier, thus reducing the effectiveness of the armor-piercing weapons. The pilots and aircrew were excited, and nearly all observed their bombs to hit. Their reports are filled with such comments as, "Aircraft next ahead hit bridge, deep red flash between funnel and bridge on port side; two exploded near ship in mid-air, another hit 'X' turret." This was aircraft G/827, the sixth to attack. "Both own bombs hit starboard side of bridge. Aircraft ahead's bombs all seemed to be on target; six to seven hits amidships seen before attacking." This was aircraft P/827, the seventh to attack. "Steady red glow amidships and smoke pouring up (aircraft F/830, 16th to attack). Twenty aircraft dived in just one minute (the 1,600-lb bomb on 830/G got hung up and did not drop. Only one aircraft was lost.

The ordnance expended in this attack totaled

- Six 1,600-lb armor-piercing (AP) (three hits)
- Twelve 500-lb medium-capacity (MC high explosive)

DETAIL OF ATTACKS

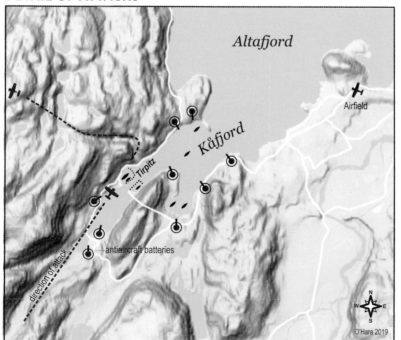

Altafjord

Airfield

Kåfjord

Tirpitz

antiaircraft batteries

direction of attack

N
W E
S

O'Hara 2019

(Created by the Author)

Tirpitz at her Kåfjord anchorage. (Peter Schenck Collection)

- Twenty-four 500-lb semi-armor-piercing (SAP) (five hits MC and SAP collectively)
- Four 600-lb A/S (two hits)

The pilots claimed 14 hits (including probables); the reality, ten hits out of 46 bombs dropped, was quite good. The damage inflicted is specified in *Tirptiz* Bomb Damage graphic, page 79. The withdrawing fighters

Ditching in the Arctic Ocean

The pilot of Hellcat B/831 Squadron was Sub-Lieutenant T. H. Hoare, RNZNR. He participated in the second strike, but when he returned to his carrier, his tailhook would not lower, apparently being damaged by gunfire. He was thus forced to ditch at sea, picking a spot near the Canadian destroyer *Algonquin*. The Canadians plucked him from the frigid water, but in very poor shape. New Zealanders had flocked to the Fleet Air Arm. In this particular operation 17 of the fighter and six of the bomber pilots were RNZNR. If Hoare was typical of the breed, then the Royal Navy did well to give them aircraft to fly. Despite the shock of ditching in the Arctic sea, Hoare quickly returned to duty and won a DSC just a month and three days later in an air operation on 6 May. He was promoted and was senior pilot of 800 Squadron at the time of Operation Dragoon, the August invasion of Southern France, and went on to command a frigate in the New Zealand navy during the Korean War.

also attacked shipping in the fjord. They strafed *V6103*, killing her captain, and set on fire *Dollart* (535 GRT) off Loppa. They also damaged *CA Larsen* (13,246 GRT), an ex-whaler serving as a repair ship.

After just five minutes the aircraft disappeared to the northwest. Splinters had wounded *Kapitän zur See* Meyer, who had been standing near the conning tower. The navigation officer, *Kapitän zur See* Wolfe Jünge, assumed command and took station at the conning tower. *Tirpitz* was under way and with smoke filling the fjord, he worried about running aground. The ship had a slight list and several fires, but the engines and the main battery were undamaged. Nonetheless, Jünge decided to cancel the exercise. *Tirpitz* was returning to her net enclosure, without benefit of a tug, when at 0633 news of another attack arrived.

The second strike repeated the route and pattern of the first attack. The planes took off at 0525, just as the first wave was attacking. There were only 18 Barracuda in this strike, because the engine on one aircraft from 829 Squadron could not be started and Q/829, which had been carrying a 1,600-lb bomb, crashed shortly after takeoff. When the planes were still 40 miles from target, they could see a pall of brown smoke over Kåfjord.

Hellcats and Wildcats came in first, diving into the smoke, which one pilot said went halfway up the surrounding hillsides. Only three aircraft located and strafed the ship; the other concentrated on the surrounding shore and hills. The Barracudas, however had better luck. One pilot noted "smoke screen over area but ship visible," another, "Smoke obscured everything except target." The German gunners on board, however, could not see the attackers. The 10.5-cm guns fired a box barrage, and the 37- and 20-mm guns shot blind through the smoke as the Barracudas dived on target. The gunners downed M/829. Aircraft H observed her squadron mate in distress, "port wing broken and on fire." Again, the pilots enthusiastically

TIRPITZ BOMB DAMAGE: Operation Tungsten, 3 April 1944

● 500-pound SAP or MC   ◉ 600-pound A/S   ● 1,600-pound A/P

GERMAN DAMAGE REPORT 1ST STRIKE

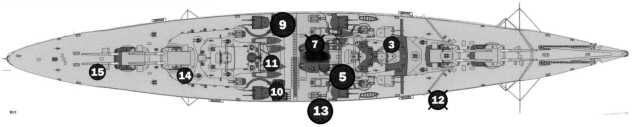

3. MC. Exploded on upper deck on the forward night control position near the main conning tower. Perforated deck inward and holed deck of the bridge steering position. Splinters caused casualties in the machine-gun crews. Otherwise slight damage.

5. Exploded on upper deck in superstructure. Destroyed the picket boat and passed through the gun platform; deflected 90 degrees inward by the upper deck and detonated in the gun room. Caused severe splinter and fire damage.

7. Hit the funnel and port side aircraft hangar. It distorted the funnel and collapsed the hangar roof. Searchlight #2 fell and funnel quadruple 20-mm mount damaged. Slight fire damage.

9. Penetrated upper deck just aft of port catapult in C/X. Exploded on lower armored deck. Caused severe damage to decks and bulkheads, demolished a port-side outboard longitudinal bulkhead, and pierced an inboard splinter bulkhead. Up to 8m of the upper deck was rolled back. Port outboard portion of the main watertight bulkhead above the lower armor deck between C/X and XI was completely destroyed and fire broke out in that area. Ducts and cabling in area destroyed or damaged. Two floatplanes destroyed by fire.

10. MC. Hit in C/X. Splinters spray only.

11. SAP. Penetrated the side of the after aircraft hangar and the superstructure deck and exploded in the wardroom. Adjoining cabins destroyed by splinters and fire. Upper deck armor bent inward.

12. Near miss near C/XVI. Caused a concussion in the ship. The outer hull was stripped open to a length of 2x1m. The adjoining tanks flooded.

13. Hit the in water opposite C/IX and penetrated the hull under the armor belt. Exploded in a fuel-oil bunker. Destroyed the inner structure of the side protection system in the area of C/IX and X, bending inward for 5m the torpedo bulkhead. Some flooding.

14. SAP. Penetrated superstructure In C/VII to starboard near after main director and exploded on upper deck in officers' aft living quarters with a strong burst of splinters. Deck dished.

15. SAP. Penetrated the upper deck on the starboard side of C/III, the main deck below and hit the armored belt which deflected it upward. There was no detonation, but it caused a heavy fire and much smoke

SECOND STRIKE

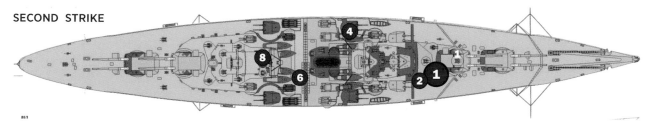

1. Hit foredeck in C/XVI. Penetrated upper deck and was stopped by the deck transverse frame. Did not explode.

2. MC. Exploded against the breakwater in C/XVI. Tore up deck planking. Splinters on all sides but otherwise no damage.

4. AP. Hit and perforated upper deck in C/XIII and disabled Port #1 105-mm mount. The blast projected downward into living quarters. Heavy fire damage

6. MC. Hit outer edge of scuppers in C/XII and exploded. Heavy splinter spray holed the degaussing apparatus but otherwise no damage.

8. SAP. Holed the after edge of the hangar and the superstructure deck and exploded in the compartment below. The sides of the compartment were blown outward. There was heavy splinter and fire damage.

saw many bombs strike target, and their reports emphasized flames covering the ship: A/831, "Large fire burning port side by bridge"; G/831, "Large fire seen amidships"; and B/831, "Fierce fire burning amidships."

The ordnance expended in this attack totaled

- Two 1,600-lb AP
- Nine 500-lb MC
- Thirty-eight 500-lb SAP
- One 600-lb A/S

Five hits were scored, one 1,600-lb dud and four 500-lb bombs, two of which exploded and started large fires. B/831 was unable to release one of its 600-lb bombs, while an electrical failure caused P/829 to drop its 500-lb SAP bombs in safe mode. On their way out the fighters heavily strafed the submarine chasers *UJ1212* in Stjernsund and *UJ1218* (ex-*Torlyn*, 247 GRT) in Kåfjord, wounding a dozen men. They were ex–fishing vessels armed with one 88-mm and six 20-mm guns each.

View of the forward control positions. (Peter Schenck Collection)

After this attack, which lasted only last a few minutes, *Tirpitz* continued her efforts to reenter her net enclosure. There was false alarm at 0719 that caused the ship to interrupt briefly her maneuvers. Casualties from the attacks were heavy, 122 men killed (including two civilian workers) and 316 wounded in all. In the attacks the ship fired 506 10.5-cm shells, 400 rounds of 37-mm, and 8,260 20-mm rounds.

On their return to the carriers the arrestor hook on one Hellcat refused to lower, and the pilot, T. H. Hoare, RNZNR, ditched alongside the Canadian destroyer *Algonquin* with an unreleased 600-lb bomb on board— the last aircraft to return to *Furious*.

In general, this attack inflicted only superficial harm to *Tirpitz*. The underwater damage required divers carrying out welding a month to repair. The blast and fire damage took longer, because so much cabling needed to be replaced. The British, on the other hand, initially believed they had done very well. *Victorious'* captain reported, "I believe *Tirpitz* now to be useless as a warship." He allowed 17 hits out of more than 30 claimed and declared this to be an absolute minimum. Moore believed *Tirpitz* "seriously damaged." The vice admiral considered a follow-up attack on the 4th but concluded it was not necessary. Cunningham pushed Fraser to order another attack, but Fraser initially refused, believing the ship severely damaged and his own aircrews exhausted.

It would have behooved the British to be as aggressive with their carriers as they possibly could have been, because, as events quickly proved, it was not easy to launch a carrier raid. On Cunningham's insistence, the same force as in Tungsten (except that *Striker* replaced *Fencer* as the antisubmarine carrier) sailed to attack *Tirpitz* on 24 April in Operation Planet. Moore canceled the operation as the ships approached the launching area, because of bad weather in Altafjord. On 15 May, in Operation Brawn, *Furious* and *Victorious*, operating without the escort carriers, launched 27 Barracudas with an escort of Corsairs and Seafires. They reached the coast to find a blanket of solid clouds over Kåfjord; they broke off and returned to their carriers. On 28 May (Operation Tiger Claw) the same force abandoned an attempt to raid Kåfjord owing to weather and instead attacked merchant shipping off Aalesund, sinking four vessels.

In two months of effort the British had been unable to deliver a carrier raid, but they weren't ready to give up.

MASCOT AND GOODWOOD

MAY–AUGUST 1944

After the failure of Operation Tiger Claw *Victorious* sailed for eastern waters, several months behind schedule. *Formidable*, coming off repairs, and the brand-new *Indefatigable* replaced her, and a long delay in carrier operations followed as these vessels absorbed new squadrons and worked up. It should also be remembered that on 6 June 1944 the Allies

Fairey Firefly being slung onto a carrier's deck. This was a two-man fleet fighter/reconnaissance aircraft that first flew in December 1941 but did not enter service until July 1944. Although used for the rest of the war, it was inferior to American types, because adapting a fighter to serve a double role made for an inferior fighter. Judging from the attire of the deck hands and the corvette in the background, this photo was taken in an Indian Ocean port. (U.S. Naval Institute photo archive)

launched the greatest amphibious operation of the war, the invasion of France at Normandy. Apparently the carriers, aircraft, and aircrews (not to mention battleships, cruisers, and destroyers) of the Home Fleet were surplus to the requirements of Operation Neptune and so could be held back to continue attacks on *Tirpitz*.

British preparations gave the Germans at Altafjord a respite—one they used to good effect. They examined what had gone wrong in April and concluded that the main problem had been a lack of warning. In response they improved communications between the radar warning stations and *Tirpitz*. They also increased the smoke-generating facilities both on board and ashore. Finally, they acted to give the 15-cm and even the 38-cm guns roles in the ship's antiaircraft defenses, devising procedures for them to fire area barrages at set distances. Even as the defenses improved, intensive work to repair the damage done by Tungsten continued. By early June the Admiralty began to be troubled by intelligence reports that *Tirpitz* was nearly ready for action. For example, the British naval attaché in Sweden forwarded reports that 400–600 men had been working day and night and that she would be ready to sail by 1 July. On 25 June a report arrived that she had been observed under way, and on 1 July another came in that *Tirpitz* had been making 20 knots during trials.

OPERATION MASCOT

Vice Admiral Moore replaced Fraser as commander-in-chief of the Home Fleet on 14 June. His first imperative was to renew the attacks on *Tirpitz*. To this end he devised Operation Mascot. He had available three fleet carriers: *Formidable*, *Indefatigable*, and the ever-faithful *Furious*. Rear Admiral R. R. McGrigor commanded the force from *Indefatigable*. The carriers and their fresh aircrews started training for Mascot on 7 July, aiming for a launch date of 17 July. They would mount a single strike that ultimately consisted of 21 Barracudas from *Formidable* (827 and 830 Squadrons) and 23 from *Indefatigable* (820 and 826 Squadrons). Top cover consisted of 18 Corsairs of 1841 Squadron flying from *Formidable*; the flak-suppression escort comprised 12 Fireflies (1770 Squadron) from *Indefatigable* and 20 Hellcats from *Furious*, which also carried 12 Seafires of 880 Squadron for combat air patrol. There were nine Swordfish for antisubmarine duties, six on *Indefatigable* and three from *Furious*. Forty-two of the Barracudas carried 1,600-lb bombs; two carried 500-lb MC (medium capacity) bombs, three each.

The fleet sortied on 14 July, with Moore on *Duke of York*. There were also four cruisers (*Kent*, *Devonshire*, *Jamaica*, and *Bellona*) and two groups of destroyers. *Matchless*, *Nubian*, *Scourge*, *Milne*, *Marne*, *Musketeer*, and *Sioux* departed a day early and refueled in the Faroes while *Volage*, *Vigilant*, *Virago*, *Verulam*, and *Algonquin* sailed with the main force. The frigates *Bulldog*, *Inman*, *Burges*, and *Hoste* screened the carriers. At 0040 Z+2 on the 17th the first fighters began to lift off. Although it was just after midnight, the sun was still shining. All the Barracudas and their escorts got airborne over the next hour, and by 0135 the strike was winging toward the arctic coast. The weather was fine, with clear skies.

Tirpitz in her Kåfjord anchorage in a shot taken from the shore, showing the torpedo nets. (Peter Schenck Collection)

Fairey Firefly ranged on the 360-foot mark about to take off. (U.S. Naval Institute photo archive)

The Germans detected the intruders at 0200, before they crossed the coast. *Tirpitz* got the word at 0204 and had all guns manned and watertight hatches secured by 0217. The smoke candles on the upper deck and the smoke generator astern were pumping out their black-and-white chemical fog by 0214, and just a minute later billowing clouds from the shore generators began to envelop the ship's stern.

When they were ten miles from Kåfjord the flight leaders saw there was 50 percent cloud over the target and that artificial smoke had already reached a height of a thousand feet. The battleship's 38-cm guns opened fire at 0219, and the first aircraft approached minutes later. The smoke was effective: only two fighters and two Barracudas spotted *Tirpitz*. The other 37 Barracudas dropped their bombs blindly over the course of 25 minutes, aiming on the flashes of the battleship's flak. The strike leader did not designate alternative targets, for which he was later criticized by Vice Admiral Moore. One Barracuda bombed a flak battery on shore and another attacked a destroyer in Langfjord. A third missed *Nordmark* with a 1,600-lb bomb. There were no hits on the battleship. Seven bombs near-missed, and one caused

Smoke Does More Than Hide

To hide *Tirpitz* from British attacks, the Germans released chlorosulfuric acid from special generators on board the ship and on the beaches and slopes around the ship. Droplets of this compound attract water and quickly forms a thick mist. British pilots reported artificial fog raising to a height of a thousand feet. Chlorosulfuric acid is irritating for people, but, at the time, it was otherwise considered harmless. Nonetheless, *Tirpitz*'s reports mention crewmen struck by respiratory problems or even poisoned by the gas. In Operation Mascot, more men were stricken by smoke than by enemy action. The men who had to fight in

this chemical soup knew it was not benign, but they probably did not know its impact would outlast their lifespans.

In April 2018 a German scientist concluded that this smoke severely affected the pine trees around Kåfjord. Claudia Hartl of the Johannes Gutenberg University in Mainz, Germany, was investigating why Scotch pine trees she and her students happened to be studying on the Kåfjord seemed stunted. In contrast to the normal-seeming tree rings from other locations in northern Norway, a few core samples the researchers took in the area showed no growth

ring or a ring that was hardly visible for the year 1945. Trees nearer to the fjord had skipped even more years. Some nearest the fjord had even stopped growing for as long as seven years, returning to normal only after 12 years. Drought or insect attacks can cause such patterns, but Scotch pines are too hardy to stop growing completely in such circumstances. The absent ring indicated that the tree was going all out to survive. Hartl [concluded] that German attempts to hide *Tirpitz* from enemy attacks by means of chemical fog left enduring evidence in the trees by stunting their growth.

A reconnaissance shot of *Tirpitz* in her Kåfjord anchorage. (U.S. Naval Institute photo archive)

"violent vibrations," according to the ship's log, but no damage.

Tirpitz expended 39 38-cm rounds, 359 of 15-cm, 1,973 of 10.5-cm, 3,967 of 37-mm, and 28,550 of 20-mm (she was now up to 80 20-mm barrels). The fire was so intense that halfway through the action Captain Jünge (who had replaced Meyer on 14 May) messaged his antiaircraft gunnery officer, "Flak must on no account run out of ammunition." For all this firing, however, only one Corsair was shot down, and one Barracuda did not make it back because of damage (it ditched next to *Formidable*, and the crew was rescued). A follow-up strike was planned, but when patches of fog appeared near the carriers Moore called it off.

Tirpitz's report of the operation reflected satisfaction: "The failure of the attack was due to the fact that the *Tirpitz* had 15 minutes warning which gave her sufficient time to man her guns, clear the ship for action, and put the various smoke screen apparatus into action. The weather conditions were particularly suitable for the use of smoke screen. The concentrated barrage from guns of all calibers screened the ship with such success as to ward off the attacker, whose task was made more difficult by this smoke screen."

The British were understandably unhappy with the results. The fighters had shot up positions up and down Altafjord, but the only ship harmed was the patrol boat *V6307* (510 GRT), which ran aground while trying to evade a strafing fighter. Moore blamed inexperienced aircrews, poor strike direction, and above all, the slow speed of the Barracuda, which gave the Germans time to prepare before the strike could arrive. It seemed that British carrier power had

regressed. Moore did not know that his force had been sighted and that it had sailed through a concentration of submarines, but he did know that every time the fleet deployed, there was a certain risk. Taking risks without reward was an unproductive policy.

Tirpitz went to sea, for the last time, on July 31 and 1 August in company with Z29, Z31, Z33, Z34, and Z39. This news reached the Admiralty, but because Murmansk convoys had been temporarily suspended the ship's operational status was not the imperative concern it would become when convoys resumed later in the year.

GOODWOOD I

Operation Goodwood comprised the final attempts to sink *Tirpitz* with carrier aviation, undertaken amid a growing imperative to send the modern fleet carriers to the Indian Ocean. Operation Goodwood I involved two groups. The first was the fleet carriers *Formidable*, *Furious*, and *Indefatigable*, along with *Duke of York*, the heavy cruisers *Devonshire* and *Berwick*, and the destroyers *Myngs*, *Sioux*, *Vigilant*, *Stord*, *Virago*, *Verulam*, *Volage*, *Kempenfelt*, and *Zambesi*. These sailed on 18 August at 0519 and were joined by the destroyers *Algonquin*, *Serapis*, *Scorpion*, *Cambrian*, *Whirlwind*, and *Wrangler* off the Faroes. The second group, which also sailed on the 18th, included the escort carriers *Nabob* and *Trumpeter*, the heavy cruiser *Kent*, and the 5th Escort Group (the frigates *Bickerton*, *Aylmer*, *Bligh*, *Keats*, and *Kemperthorn*). Once again, the FAA squadrons had been shuffled between carriers and their strike capabilities enhanced. *Formidable*'s Corsairs (1841 and 1842 Squadrons) had received dive-bombing training, and the escort carriers had between them 20 Grumman TBF 1-C Avenger IIs and ten FM-1 Wildcats. The Avengers were a new element to the mix. They would carry mines and drop them alongside *Tirpitz* and in the entrance to Kåfjord.

The plan called for the two groups to unite and launch their strike on 21 August to cover Convoy JW 59's passage. However, weather caused a one-day delay. At 1150 on the 22nd the strike force finally cleared the decks. It consisted of:

- 32 Barracudas
- 24 Corsairs
- 11 Fireflies
- 9 Hellcats
- 8 Seafires

Because the Avengers could not land with the mines still attached, there were only enough mines for one strike, and conditions over the target were uncertain, McGrigor did not want to take a chance of a failed effort. In this he was undoubtedly right, because when the strike force crossed the coast it encountered solid cloud cover. Faced with this obstruction, the Barracudas and Corsairs, according to their orders, turned back.

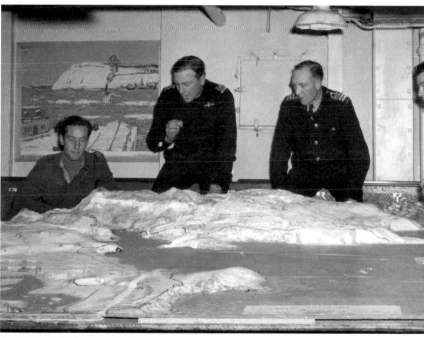

On HMS *Nabob* planning the attack. (Courtesy Canadian DND)

Nabob down by the stern. (Courtesy Canadian DND)

The other aircraft continued. The Seafires strafed Banak airfield outside Alta and the Kolvick seaplane base, where they destroyed two of the battleship's floatplanes. They also conducted a diversionary attack against Hammerfest at 1310 and shot up *U-965*, wounding the captain and 11 other men. The Fireflies and Hellcats, meanwhile, pestered *Tirpitz*. This time there was little warning, and the attenuated strike arrived before smoke had covered the battleship. The Fireflies began their strafing runs at 1249, and the Hellcats, each armed with a single 500-lb SAP bomb, started diving at 1251. Despite the advantages of surprise and relatively good visibility, all bombs missed the target. The fighters strafed and drove ashore two ferry barges, causing many casualties. The antiaircraft battery "Tangen" likewise suffered heavy casualties. *Tirpitz* claimed eight aircraft shot down, the land batteries 14, and the auxiliary ships another two. The actual cost was one Hellcat and one Seafire. For their part the British claimed one hit on *Tirpitz*.

Nabob's only participation in the operation so far had been launching four Wildcats for fleet defense. During the afternoon of the 22nd she had just recovered her Wildcats and, in company with *Kent* and *Trumpeter*, was withdrawing west to refuel her screen when she was shaken by a violent explosion. *U-354*, hurrying north to intercept JW 59, had happened on the escort carrier force by chance. The acoustic conditions were poor for detecting submarines, and she easily penetrated the screening frigates of the 5th Escort Group, commanded by one of the Royal Navy's antisubmarine aces, Captain Donald MacIntyre (who was in the wardroom playing bridge at the time of the attack). The submarine fired an FaT pattern-running torpedo at 1716 that hit the escort carrier astern and blasted a hole 30 by 50 feet. At first it seemed the ship would settle by the stern and sink. But her engine room bulkhead held, and she was able

On *Nabob*'s tilting deck. *Bickerton* in distress is to the right. (Courtesy Canadian DND)

to restart her engines. *U-354* fired a second torpedo to finish off *Nabob* but hit the frigate *Bickerton*. The frigate lost 40 men and was dispatched by a British destroyer so the rest of the group could screen the slowly moving carrier. In a feat of outstanding seamanship on the part of Captain H. N. Lay, RCN, the carrier made it back to Scapa Flow. (She was never repaired. There were too many brand-new "baby flattops" coming out of American shipyards for the effort to be worthwhile.) She was the largest ship damaged in the quest to sink *Tirpitz*.

GOODWOOD II

At 1830 on the same day *Indefatigable* flew off six Hellcats and eight Fireflies for another nuisance raid (referred to as "teasing" raids in the British reports). They arrived over the target at 1910 and in an attack lasting until 1927 achieved complete surprise. Once again, the Hellcats scored near misses but no hits. The ship lost one man killed and ten wounded. The fighters also attacked the tankers *Jeverland* (seven wounded and minor damage), *Nordmark* (a near miss and two wounded), the supply ship *Neumark* (one dead and two wounded), and the patrol boat *Vp6504*. The auxiliary warship suffered

one death and 21 wounded and claimed to have shot down four aircraft, earning a "well done" from Dönitz. *Tirpitz* expended (first attack/second attack) 62/13 rounds of 38-cm, 363/124 of 15-cm, plus 10.5-cm, 37-mm, and 20-mm. The battleship claimed four British aircraft shot down in the second attack, land batteries four or five.

GOODWOOD III

On the evening of 22 August, the escort carriers withdrew, covered by *Formidable* and *Furious*. *Indefatigable* lingered, intending to launch a strike against Langfjord on the 23rd, but the weather did not cooperate. On 24 August, after the return of *Formidable* and *Furious*, the conditions were, according to the Admiralty War Diary, "nearly perfect," and the British sent against *Tirpitz* and Altafjord:

- 33 Barracudas (all with 1,600-lb bombs)
- 24 Corsairs (five armed with a single 1,000-lb AP bomb)
- Ten Fireflies
- Ten Hellcats (all with 500-lb AP bombs)
- 8 Seafires

A deck load of Corsairs on board HMS *Formidable*. The ship following off the port quarter is a *Kent*-subclass heavy cruiser. (U.S. Naval Institute photo archive)

The planes were en route by 1500. They had been launched from farther south in an attempt to achieve surprise, but this had the opposite effect. German radar picked them up at 1535 at a range of 63 miles and alerted *Tirpitz* by 1541. The Hellcats and Fireflies attacked at 1600 through a smoke screen already well developed, although portions forward and starboard were still visible. As the war diary noted, "The defense of the *Tirpitz* was carried out by guns of all calibers and with smoke screen. The preliminary time of warning of thirteen minutes was sufficient to establish the total condition of water-tightness."

The Hellcats finally got a hit, landing a 500-lb SAP bomb squarely on one of the more heavily armored areas in the ship, the top of B turret. This destroyed the quadruple 20-mm mount located there and damaged the range finder but otherwise did no harm. Flak accounted for two Hellcats.

The Barracudas and Corsairs arrived two minutes later to find the smoke screen complete. They attacked nonetheless, and more quickly and with greater coordination than in the July operation. The bombs were well distributed and dropped from the proper heights. As one Barracuda crewman recalled, "The pull out of the dive in the smoke with mountains around us and many other aircraft above was a feature of the occasion which has stuck in the memory." Another pilot: "*Tirpitz* completely obscured by an effective smoke-screen, bombs dropped blindly and results not observed." Nonetheless, one 1,600-lb bomb struck a few feet to port of the bridge. It penetrated five decks before stopping in No. 4 Switchboard Room. Fortunately for the Germans, the fuze was defective and, in any case, the bomb was only half-filled with explosives (the Germans were not the only ones with quality-control issues in their ammunition). The Hellcats claimed one certain and one probable hit, the Corsairs one possible hit, and the Barracudas one possible.

As always, the fighters rampaged up and down the fjords, strafing *Vp6502* and *Vp6510* as well as a minesweeper and the radar station on Loppa Island. A bomb aimed at *Tirpitz* hit an ammunition dump ashore instead and caused a great explosion. Battery "Talvik" had three guns put out of action.

Flak shot down one Corsair, and another ditched on its return to its carrier. The Germans expended 72 rounds of 38-cm, 510 of 15-cm, and 40 percent of the remaining ammunition supply for the other calibers. Eight men were killed and 13 wounded. The damage had been very light, although if the 1,600-lb bomb had functioned correctly, it could have caused serious harm.

In his report Captain Jünge wrote, "The attack on the 24.8.1944 was undoubtedly the heaviest and most determined so far experienced. The English showed great skill and dexterity in flying. . . . During the dive-bombing, fighter planes attacked the land Flak batteries which, in comparison with earlier attacks, suffered heavy losses. The fact that the armour-piercing bomb of more than 1,540 pounds did not explode must be considered an exceptional stroke of luck, as the effects of that explosion would have been immeasurable." The SKL War Diary noted that the "the serious consumption of ammunition makes it necessary to bring up urgently supplies of anti-aircraft artillery ammunition as exhaustion of all ammunition must be dreaded if a further attack is made."

GOODWOOD IV

The results seemed more promising than before, and the British were eager to try again. *Furious* needed to withdraw but sent a pair of Barracudas and a pair of Seafires to *Indefatigable* to replace losses. After refueling their screen, the two modern carriers, supported by *Duke of York*, *Devonshire*, and a dozen destroyers, prepared to launch a fourth effort. However, the weather closed in, and it was not until 29 August that they were able to send their aircraft aloft, and even then the forecast was marginal. At 1530 they launched

- 26 Barracudas with 1,600-lb bombs
- 17 Corsairs (two with 1,000-lb bombs)
- 10 Fireflies
- 7 Hellcats (4 with 500-lb target-indicator bombs and 3 with 500-lb AP bombs)
- 7 Seafires

The target-indicating Hellcats were an innovation. The British had recognized that the Barracudas were too slow to reach the target before the smoke was in place. They were, however, the only aircraft that could carry truly damaging ordnance; using faster aircraft to mark targets was an attempt to make them effective.

On this day, however, the Germans were not to be caught napping. Their radar had been tracking British air activity over the carriers and picked up the Seafires heading for Hammerfest. A full-scale alert was issued forty-five minutes before the main attack (which lasted from 1702 to 1727). As a result the Hellcats encountered smoke denser than ever before and were unable to mark the target accurately, forcing the British once again to bomb blindly. They claimed two hits, but in fact the best they did was a near miss. It sprayed splinters that damaged an ammunition hoist for a 10.5-cm mounting and wounded six men. The fighters strafed small ships and targets ashore but did no significant damage, aside from a bomb hit on a fuel storage tank that cost the Germans 350 tons of precious fuel oil. *Z34* and *Z31* reported "numerous gun hits." The Germans expended 54 38-cm rounds, 161 15-cm rounds, and 20 percent of their other calibers of antiaircraft ammunition. They downed one Firefly and one Corsair, not 13 as claimed. Two Barracudas made poor landings because of flak damage, one of which had to be pushed over the side.

Admiral Moore recognized that *Tirpitz* remained operational and so sent *Formidable* and *Duke of York* with six destroyers north to cover Convoy RA 59A, which had left Murmansk on 28 August. *Indefatigable* was running short on fuel and with *Scorpion*, *Algonquin*, and *Wrangler* departed for Scapa Flow on 29 August. *Formidable* with *Scourge* and the Norwegian destroyer *Stord* followed a day later, and the rest of the force turned for home on 1 September. In reviewing the Goodwood operation Rear Admiral McGrigor identified the weather and the slow speed of the Barracudas as the major reason better results had not been obtained. Moore basically endorsed these findings. Both admirals were surprised that German fighters had failed to defend the ship. The local air command had in fact requested fighters, but the Luftwaffe supreme command had turned it down.

The lessons learned in Goodwood might have been useful had the British tried another major operation, but the need for the modern carriers in the Far East was urgent and, in fact, even before the operation was over *Formidable* had orders to depart for that theater no later than 10 September. In five months of effort the British carriers had failed to knock *Tirpitz* out of the war.

THE TALLBOY ATTACKS
SEPTEMBER–NOVEMBER 1944

The Germans diligently repaired the damage the Goodwood raids had inflicted on *Tirpitz*, and by 15 September 1944 the ship was once again ready for sea trials. However, time was running out: in early September the Royal Air Force began considering how to attack *Tirpitz*. It had been two and a half years since the RAF's last attempt on the battleship, and the effectiveness of bombers up to that point had been zero. In the intervening period the same aircraft types were flying in frontline service, but the ordnance the heavy bombers had been adapted to carry had become far more potent.

Because Altafjord was beyond the range of bombers based in Britain, the British secured Soviet permission to launch a raid from Russia. They eventually settled on Yagodnik Field, on an island in the Dvina River south of Archangel, 550 nautical miles from the target. This was the site of a Russian naval air station that had a 5,000-foot

Avro Lancaster Bomber. The type entered service in February 1942 and enjoyed a successful career as the premier night heavy bomber in British service. It served in the RAF up through 1953. (Courtesy Canadian DND)

Tallboy bomb waiting to be loaded into the Lancaster in the background. The open bomb-bay doors show the length of the bay, a feature that enabled the Lancaster to accommodate such a large weapon. (Courtesy Canadian DND)

"tundra and sand" runway that the planners considered more suitable than fields around Murmansk closer to the target. They initially envisioned bombing on the way in from Britain and landing in Russia to refuel, but on 11 September the planners decided that because of the vagaries of the weather, the best chance of success would be to have the aircraft start and end their mission in Russia. The RAF assigned two of its elite squadrons to the task: the 617 and the 9 Squadrons, both flying adapted Lancasters I's, which had bulged bomb bays to accommodate the 12,000-lb Medium Capacity, or "Tallboy," bomb. The British believed that if dropped from sufficient height this weapon could penetrate the battleship's armored decks right down to the keel and perhaps all the way through, to explode just beneath the ship with catastrophic effect. The RAF's 617 Squadron, which had successfully attacked the Möhne and Eder Dams in May 1943 and was thereafter known as the "Dambusters," employed a new stabilized, automatic bomb sight to improve accuracy.

OPERATION PARAVANE

Eighteen Lancasters from each squadron, a photo-reconnaissance Mosquito, and two Liberators carrying supplies departed Britain on 10 September on the 1,350-nm flight to Yagodnik. One Lancaster had to turn back early, but 23 arrived early on 11 September in a driving rain with "10/10ths" cloud cover. During the day another seven straggled in from other landing sites. Five aircraft had had to force-land and been lost to the mission because of damage. Weather dictated the pace of operations, and it was not until 15 September that 27 Lancasters finally took off. Twenty-one aircraft carried the 12,000-lb MC bombs, and the other six carried a dozen 400-lb JW II "Johnny Walker" buoyant bombs. These were intended to fall into the water and then rise and sink, rise and sink, for up to two hours (hence "buoyant"), ideally contacting a ship's bottom and exploding before time expired. This raid was the Johnny Walker's first operational use, and Bomber Command rightfully considered it a long-shot weapon. The 617 Squadron's commander, Wing Commander J. B. Tait, led the attack.

The British had hoped that approaching from the southeast would decrease enemy reaction time, but once again radar gave the Germans ample warning of the attack; smoke generation started eight minutes before the aircraft—approaching in tight groups of six—

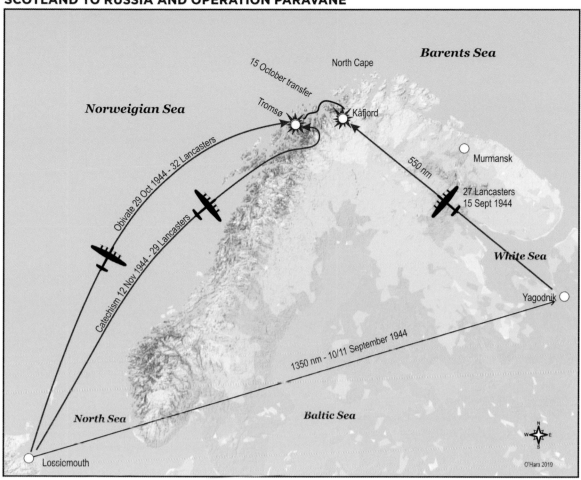

Barents Sea

North Cape

15 October transfer

Tromsø · Kåfjord

Norweigian Sea

Obivate 29 Oct 1944 - 32 Lancasters

Catechism 12 Nov 1944 - 29 Lancasters

550 nm

Murmansk

27 Lancasters
15 Sept 1944

White Sea

Yagodnik

1350 nm - 10/11 September 1944

North Sea

Baltic Sea

Lossiemouth

O'Hara 2019

(Created by the Author)

arrived. The first group, led by Tait, encountered a well-developed screen, but the tip of *Tirpitz'* mast marked her location and provided a point of aim. Tait landed his bomb on target and other aircraft of his group achieved several near misses. The other groups missed by as much as a mile, their accuracy being affected by the poor visibility and the curtains of steel that the ship's weapons and the adjoining batteries flung into the air.

Tait's bomb landed just forward of the anchor chain lockers and passed through the hull to explode below the keel. The blast ripped a hole of 32 by 48 feet and basically destroyed the ship's bow as far aft as A turret. *Tirpitz* flooded forward and settled by eight feet; she had to transfer fuel aft and flood her aft wing compartments to compensate, ending up with 1,500 tons of water on board. The near misses caused vibration and whip effects that rendered the engines unserviceable. The two squadrons dropped 17 Tallboys in this action. The other four (and one aircraft armed with the 400-lb Johnny Walker bomb) aborted rather than drop blind.

The Tallboy Bomb

ADAPTED FROM *BATTLESHIPS: AXIS AND NEUTRAL BATTLESHIPS IN WORLD WAR II*, BY GARZKE AND DULIN, NAVAL INSTITUTE PRESS

The "tallboys" were bombs especially designed for deep penetration into the ground and maximum earth shock. They had an overall weight of 12,024 pounds, contained 5,200 pounds of Torpex, and could penetrate 12 feet of reinforced concrete when dropped from 15,000 feet. This was a new weapon, developed in 1943 and coming into service in June 1944 against a railroad tunnel south of Normandy. It also proved effective against targets like V-weapon sites and two thousand were ordered that month. The bomb was 21 feet long and 38 inches in diameter and each one was handmade in a very labor-intensive process. For this reason they were not considered expendable weapons and aircraft were instructed to avoid bombing without a good target and to bring the bomb back to base if the odds of obtaining a hit were considered too poor.

Another view of the Tallboy on a loading trolley.
(Courtesy Canadian DND)

Konteradmiral Peters, the recently appointed commander of the 1st Battle Group, was on board during the attack. After the war he told British interrogators that it was "the worst air attack he had so far experienced." He thought that 30 to 40 aircraft were involved in the strike. "A smoke screen was put up and warning was given by shore radar installations which also directed *Tirpitz'* main armament for putting up barrages in way of attacking aircraft. In all 134 guns were firing in defence of the ship, including the 38 cm. main armament." Despite the damage, only one man was killed and five wounded. Ironically, the fatality was reportedly a crewman incarcerated in a forward cell. He was under a sentence of death for desertion.

After this successful strike the bombers returned to Yagodnik, where they refueled before flying to Britain the next day. They did not at first know whether their attack had succeeded, and initial photo reconnaissance was inconclusive. On 1 October, however, a reliable Norwegian agent radioed an encouraging report that there was a hole above and below the waterline so large a motorboat could go through it.

Tirpitz was indeed finished as a warship, but the German command decided she could still serve as a floating battery to defend Tromsø to the south.

For her move workers welded stringers across the starboard side to hold the bow rigid. Three tugs, five destroyers, the flak ships *Nymphe* and *Thetis*, and four

The Fatal Hit

ADAPTED FROM *BATTLESHIPS: AXIS AND NEUTRAL BATTLESHIPS IN WORLD WAR II*, BY GARZKE AND DULIN, NAVAL INSTITUTE PRESS

A "tallboy" struck the forecastle, passed through the bow overhang and exploded in the seabed. A vast amount of water and mud shot up on a tall column, which rolled back the overhanging portion of the upper deck on its way. A 30-meter section of the bow was devastated by the explosion. The bottom plating was ruptured or buckled for approximately 15 meters abaft the heavily damaged forward end. Subsequent inspection of the ship revealed that the longitudinal bulkheads in the forward part of the ship had sustained tears in the plating and the connection between the bulkheads and the shell had been severed. The bow was flooded from the stem to a point 36 meters aft below the upper platform, and flooding occurred for almost 24 meters on that deck (some 800 to 1,000 tons). Damage in the bow area further weakened some of the side frames that had been badly strained by the mine attack in September 1943. The anchor windlass was put out of action, and there was light shock-response damage to the main propulsion turbine foundations, but heavy damage to sensitive fire-control instruments. Fuel oil and lubricating oil tanks were also damaged.

minesweepers accompanied *Tirpitz* in this, her last voyage at sea. Her speed was no more than nine knots. The ship might have been safer in Altafjord, but Finland had just signed an armistice with the Soviet Union on 19 September, and there were plans to evacuate the Alta area in the face of mounting Soviet pressure.

The ship's new berthing place off Håkoy Island was selected to give her batteries a wide field of fire, particularly up the fjord. According to charts, the bottom was sand over rock and there was a uniform depth that would put six feet of water beneath the ship at low tide. However, even before the ship arrived, Captain Jünge worried that the safeguards against sinking or capsizing seemed very questionable. He was right: soundings showed six feet of water beneath her bow and stern (at low water) but 20 feet under the keel midships. In other words, the ship was to be anchored over a hole in the seabed. The fact that there was mud rather than rock beneath the sand was not immediately apparent. Rather than move the ship to a safer anchorage to the south, one that would partially block the lines of fire up the fjord, command decided to decrease the depth of the water beneath the ship, a job that would require a million cubic feet of fill. This work did not begin until 2 November. In an inquest after her sinking the Admiral Polar Coast, *Vizeadmiral* Nordmann, suggested that the ship's crew had not positioned the vessel correctly and that the maximum (high tide) depth was actually 50 feet. In the different accounts of these matters there are discrepancies as to the depth (tidal range at Tromsø was no more than ten feet), but it is clear that *Tirpitz* moored in water too deep for her own good.

Allied air reconnaissance was quick to notice that *Tirpitz* was no longer at Kåfjord, but at first it was not clear where she had gone, there being no convoys at sea for her to attack. On 16 October the new carrier *Implacable* sailed with 21 Barracudas and 11 Fireflies. The Fireflies were flown off to search for *Tirpitz* in the Tromsø area, and they duly found her on the 18th. *Implacable*'s captain wanted to send his Barracudas in to strike her, but permission was refused because there were not enough fighters available to fly top cover, flak suppression, and fleet protection simultaneously.

Captured German Documents

EXTRACT FROM REPORT N.I.D. 24/T34/45.

It was repeatedly observed that the aircraft closed in before releasing their bombs. Immediately after doing so the groups broke up again. The aircraft then turned off singly in various directions. Those still carrying bombs repeated their attack at once either singly or forming up into twos and threes as they came in from different directions. The attacks were principally made in the direction of the fjord (i.e., parallel to the length of the ship).

As a result of this heavy attack, very serious damage was caused to the ship. The bow was hit and from hawsepipes to forward turret was almost completely destroyed. The main engines were also damaged by the vibration. It was estimated that repairs, if they could be carried out without interruption, would take at least nine months.

It was eventually decided at a conference on 23rd September, 1944, at which the C. in C. and Naval War Staff were present, that it was no longer possible to make the *Tirpitz* ready for sea and action again. It was therefore considered that in order to preserve the remaining fighting efficiency of the ship, she should be used as a reinforcement to the defences in the Polar Area. For this purpose *Tirpitz* was to be moved as soon as possible to the area west of Lyngenfjord, moored in shallow water and brought into operation as a floating battery.

The operation of moving the *Tirpitz* was carried out on 15th October, 1944. A berth was selected near Tromsø–Håkoy net enclosure. The ship was protected against underwater attacks and aerial torpedoes by means of a double net barrage. Shore anti-aircraft guns and smoke-screen units were moved from Ka Fjord to Tromsø. As the ship was only partially seaworthy, the crew, particularly engine-room personnel, was decreased. It was found that there were varying depths of water at the selected berth; in particular there was a hollow below the midship section. Too many difficulties would have arisen if the ship were to be moved again, so it was decided to fill in the hollow till the water was 2 meters deep below the keel. Work was commenced by dredgers on 1st November, and by 12th November about 14,000 cubic metres had been filled in at both sides below the midship section.

Tirpitz at her anchorage off Håkoy Island. Although the image is poor, the antitorpedo net is visible. This position was much more exposed than the one at Kåfjord, in part because the location was chosen to allow the ship to serve as a battery rather than to protect her from air attack. (Public Domain)

OPERATION OBVIATE

The big problem with the Tromsø area from the German point of view was that it was in range, if barely, of British airfields. Once again, 617 and 9 Squadrons were assigned to strike the battleship, this time in her new berth. The Lancasters each had its mid-upper turret and some armor removed and an extra gas tank fitted. Their 1,460-hp Rolls-Royce Merlin 22 engines were swapped out for the 1,620-hp 24 model to give them the range and power to reach their target.

The forecast for 29 October seemed to favor an attack, so 32 Lancasters—all armed with Tallboys—took off from Lossiemouth in Scotland at 0300. German radar picked up the incoming bombers in time for the antiaircraft batteries to be manned and the watertight doors secured. There was no smoke, but the wind had shifted and low clouds obscured the target from the minimum release point of 13,000 feet. Some aircrews made as many as four runs each, but no bombs struck the target. The nearest fell 50 feet to port of the

Painting by Gerald Coulson depicting a Lancaster attack at Tromsø. (U.S. Naval Institute photo archive)

UNITED STATES NAVAL INSTITUTE

rudders. Flak damaged one aircraft, which had to make an emergency landing in Sweden.

The near miss split the port side plating aft and rendered the glands at the end of the port propeller shaft no longer watertight, permitting slow flooding along 115 feet of the port side aft. The concussion also bent the port shaft, damage that would require a dry dock to repair. With the ship thus immobilized the Germans started to refer to her as *Die Schwimmende Batterie* (floating battery) *Tirpitz*.

On 2 November the dredgers got to work filling in the holes beneath the keel. The bombs that had fallen around *Tirpitz* at a distance had revealed that the seabed in her anchorage was mud, not rock, but it was too late to move the ship. Two days later Captain Jünge was recalled to Berlin, against his wishes. His chief gunnery officer, *Kapitän zur See* Robert Weber, became the new commanding officer.

OPERATION CATECHISM

After Obviate, Ultra confirmed that *Tirpitz*' sailing days were finally over. There were no Allied plans to land troops in Tromsø, so clearly the ship was no longer a threat. In fact, given the commitment in men and energy her existence had until then entailed, it might seem more beneficial to the Allied cause just to leave her be. But by this time *Tirpitz* was more than a warship—she was a symbol. The British felt they had their foot on the German neck, and they wanted to destroy every vestige of Nazi power, apparently whether of military significance or not.

On 12 November, at 0300, 29 Lancasters of 617 and 9 Squadrons started taking off from Lossiemouth. The aircraft made their way to a rendezvous point south of Tromsø. Individually, exploiting known gaps in German radar coverage, hoping to evade radar detection longer. Nonetheless, the first detections were made at 0738 and came in to *Tirpitz* at 0800. The Luftwaffe commander at Bardufoss was alerted that an air raid was possible. The Lancasters came together between 0830 and 0845, and the strike was definitely identified as such by 0905, when the bombers were still 75 miles away. *Tirpitz* was already at action stations. The first aircraft was sighted as a speck in the sky at 0927 about 25 miles to the southeast. The smoke generators ashore were pumping out their dense, noxious product, but they were not as effective in the anchorage's open waters as they had been in the steep and narrow Kåfjord. Turrets A and

ATTACKS AT HÅKOY ISLAND

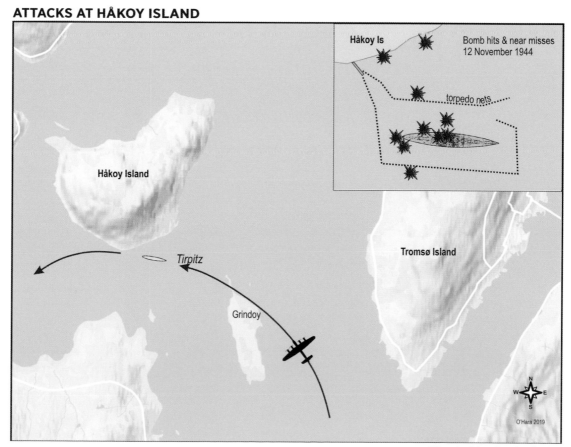

(Created by the Author)

Sailors gazing up at the remains of a propeller shaft. (*Signal Magazine*, Enrico Cernuschi)

The wreck in 1947, immediately before salvage work commenced. This gives a good idea of the size of the ship. (Aldo Fraccaroli Collection, USMM)

Report of *Oberleutnant zur See* Fässbender

ADAPTED FROM *LAST YEAR OF THE KRIEGSMARINE*, BY V. E. TARRANT, NAVAL INSTITUTE PRESS

12/11/44: Clear, cloudless, very good visibility. Wind SW 1-2. Sunrise 0930. High Water 1100.

0800: W/T signal reporting penetration of one Lancaster in Bodo area. As penetrations of four-engine bombers are likely to have special significance, a clarification of this report was required from the main observer post.

0815: Penetration of 3 Lancasters reported near Mosjoen,

course east (tactical time 0738). On account of this report an attack by four-engined formations similar to that on 29th October is anticipated, as the circumstances are similar—time of day, weather and approach. Telephonic consultation between AA gunnery officer and officer-in-charge of main observer post for the purpose of clarifying the air situation and securing fighter protection.

0825: Another 4 Lancasters reported, course NE in Mosjoen area. It therefore strengthened our suspicions that the enemy intended to attack. . . . Fighter protection requested from divisional control at Bardufoss. Inquiry made regarding strength and course of formation. Fighter protection not yet granted up to the present. Up to 0840 no further report on air situation. AA alarm given as a precaution.

B opened fire at 0938 at a range of 27,000 yards. The 15-cm and 10.5-cm guns joined in at 19,000 yards. The British bombers came on, closing formation as they neared the target.

As before, Wing Commander Tait led the first group, and he released his bomb at 0941. His group scored two direct hits. There was a near miss near the bow. During the next three minutes the bombers achieved another hit and another damaging near miss. There was massive flooding, and at 0945 Captain Weber ordered the lower decks to be evacuated. Steam and smoke from the first hit obscured the target for the later groups, but more than half the bombs fell within 250 yards of target. By this this the ship's list was 40 degrees to port. As the bombers disappeared, without casualties, the list continued to increase. At 0950 it was nearly 70 degrees when the C turret magazine exploded, blowing the turret from its barbette. By 0952 the ship had capsized completely. Had the anchorage been as shallow as originally intended, and the bottom rock, the ship would have remained upright. Many men were trapped inside, and the final toll varies according to source from 902 to 1,204 men killed.

Bomb Damage: 12 November

ADAPTED FROM *BATTLESHIPS: AXIS AND NEUTRAL BATTLESHIPS IN WORLD WAR II*, BY GARZKE AND DULIN, NAVAL INSTITUTE PRESS

The damage caused by the bomb hit near the catapult on the port side was severe; the bomb went through all decks and armor and detonated in a filled wing tank near the torpedo bulkhead of the port engine room. Shell plating and waterline armor in the immediate area completely disappeared for approximately one-third of the ship's breadth and the bilge keel and ship's bottom plating were missing up to the cooling water discharge sea chest. The longitudinal extent of this damage was over four main watertight compartments (10, 11, 12 and 13). The torpedo bulkhead was bent inboard and torn open; the remaining portion of the demolished shell plating was spread outboard. The engine room, boiler auxiliary engine room, two boiler rooms, and electrical generator room number 4 on the port side, including all spaces beneath the lower armor deck and to the port side of the centerline flooded immediately. The explosion also destroyed the watertight integrity of the adjoining spaces on the upper deck. . . . The near misses threw a great quantity of shrapnel and water against the port side aft from the stern to the funnel. Small leaks through the shrapnel holes contributed to the subsequent port list. Although seven bombs fell within the torpedo nets, ten craters were clearly visible from the air at various distances on the port side of the ship. There was no report of any bombs exploding anywhere along the starboard side.

0855: Air Raid Alert. Also for Tromso.

0902: Ship made ready for action. Stand to.

0905: Open formation of about 20 to 25 aircraft sighted 120 km to the south. From now on intentions of attack on *Tirpitz* are obvious. All eyes keep watch on the formation. First its course is NE, then it turns at a distance of about 70 km to make a direct approach. From the time of the first sighting, fighter protection has been requested continuously via the main observer post. About 0912 a second formation is sighted in the south and simultaneously reported by the main observer post. The formations are flying at a height of about 2,500 to 3,000 meters. Upon repeated requests for fighter protection a signal is received about 0915 as follows: "Enemy formation over Bardufoss, therefore impossible for fighters to take off."

0915: Captain to all: "Fighters have been requested."

0925: One fighter reported to have taken-off; shortly afterwards more fighters.

0927: Captain to all: "We are expecting a heavy air attack and the ship's company of *Tirpitz* will again fulfill its duty and prepare a hot reception for the four-engined bombers."

0927: Smoke flares sighted from first formation at about 40 km distance. The formation forms up into groups for the attack.

0940: Forward main armament opens fire at about 210 hm

The wreck postwar being salvaged by a Norwegian/German consortium. Salvage work started in 1948 and continued to 1957. The steel is particularly valuable because it was produced before the atomic-bomb tests and thus is not contaminated with traces of radiation. It is also valuable for sentimental and historical reasons. Today an item like a folding pocket knife produced with steel salvaged from *Tirpitz* sells for more than ten times as much as one forged with ordinary steel. (*War at Sea*, Jürgen Rowher)

[hectometers, thus 21,000 meters]. At about 150 hm range secondary armament and heavy anti-aircraft also open fire. The bursts of the first main armament salvo were low, the range was good. In spite of well-directed secondary armament and main anti-aircraft fire, the aircraft proceed steadily on their course of attack. The medium and light anti-aircraft guns came into operation mostly only after the bombs had been dropped. Upon the approach of the formation, one was observed to be shot down.

0942: A stick of bombs of the heaviest caliber fall in close proximity mostly inside the net enclosure. Two direct hits are observed on the port side, one on the aircraft catapult and one beside 'B' turret. The ship is drenched by high water columns, and a few second later lists heavily to port. From the effect of the first hit there is a marked decrease in defensive fire, due to casualties in materiel and personnel. In spite of the increasing list the fire from the heavy and light anti-aircraft guns is kept up until shortly before the capsizing. Shortly after the first bomb-hits the order was given by the repair party control to correct the trim by flooding.

0945: Ship listing about 30 to 40 degrees to port. Order from Captain: "Abandon lower deck." Shortly afterward Captain to Gunnery officer: "Fire everything possible."

0950: Ship listing 60 to 70 degrees to port. 'C' turret blows up with a tongue of fire. Cause unknown. At this time there were still three aircraft over the ship. Bomb-hits near 'C' were not observed. It is supposed that the explosion was caused by the ammunition catching fire. List increasing quickly.

0952: The ship capsizes to port and is lying at an angle of about 135 degrees. A small number of the crew were able to remain on the capsizing ship. The rest of the men on the upper deck tried to reach land by swimming or with the assistance of floats or objects drifting around. After about 15 minutes the first rescue vessels arrived.

The Luftwaffe Fails to Intervene

It may seem remarkable that *Tirpitz* was attacked by aircraft 40 times between 1940 and 1944 and not once did German fighters rise in her defense. As outlined in the Fässbender report, they were requested early and often during the 12 November attack but failed to contest the skies over Tromsø.

The German air force base was at Bardufoss, ten minutes' flying time south of Tromsø. On 8 November a *Gruppe* (10th Squadron) from III./JG 5, with mostly rookie pilots flying Bf.109s, reinforced the 9th Squadron equipped with Fw/190s, which was already there. In overall command was Major Heinrich Ehrler, an ace with 199 kills. With these reinforcements there may have been as many as 24 fighters at Bardufoss when the Catechism raid began. Although the 9th Squadron was at three minutes' notice, it could not respond directly to a call for help from a navy observation post; its orders had to come up along the chain of command. Apparently these orders arrived at 0918, but a map plotting error delayed Ehrler's takeoff in a Bf.109 until 0923. The rest of the squadron was delayed following him by a Ju.88 (or Ju.52) coming in to land. Thus, the ace and *Gruppe* commander started north alone. He later claimed to have conducted a wide search but failed to see any enemy bombers. Meanwhile

18 other fighters took off, all between 0932 and 0942, and orbited the airbase awaiting leaders (the commander of the 10th Squadron was last one aloft). What happened then to the fighters is hard to decipher. One report says they flew to the Norwegian/Swedish border. Another has it that several planes arrived at Tromsø but saw no enemy aircraft (one pilot did report a huge ship laying hull upward). Another report has it that the novice pilots of the 10th Squadron flew to Alta. One aircraft apparently did chase the Lancaster that had been damaged by flak into Swedish airspace. It seems clear that the fighters delayed takeoff past the time when they could have assisted *Tirpitz*. Ehrler was court-martialed and sentenced to three years' imprisonment. This caused a stir, and he was later exonerated—partially on testimony by his subordinates that the squadron had not received accurate information regarding the ship's location(!). Ehrler was assigned to a Me.262 fighter squadron. He died in 1945 when he rammed his aircraft into an American bomber, his 208 credited kill. As one author states in summarizing the activities of III./JG 5 on that date: "Overall, the confusion of reported and alleged messages has contrived to muddy the waters of understanding—possibly deliberately to protect the guilty."

**The ship's distinctive and powerful profile.
(Peter Schenk Collection)**

After four years of attacks, after stupendous efforts, *Tirpitz* had finally been put off the board. The British had deployed their entire range of air and naval assets to attack the single enemy ship. They had employed new weapons like chariots, X-boats, the Tallboy, and Johnny Walker bombs. They deployed as many as five carriers in a task force to attack *Tirpitz*, they suspended traffic to the Soviet Union along sea lanes threatened by *Tirpitz*, and they delayed moving assets to the Pacific—all because of *Tirpitz*. The ship may have had a quiet career in comparison to the short, violent life of her sister *Bismarck*. But acting as a threat, as an expression of potential power, she was the most cost-effective weapon deployed by the German navy during the war. Indeed, few other weapons in the history of warfare can claim an impact approaching that exercised by this one ship.

World of Warships is a free-to-play naval warfare-themed massively multiplayer online game produced and published by Wargaming. Like their other games, *World of Tanks* (WoT) and *World of Warplanes* (WoWP); players take control of historic vehicles to battle others in player-vs-player or play cooperatively against bots or in a player versus environment (PvE) battle mode. *World of Warships* (WoWs) was originally released for on PC in 2015, the PlayStation 4 and Xbox One console versions, titled *World of Warships: Legends*, followed in 2019 and released on the PlayStation 5 and Xbox Series X/S in April 2021.

Developed by Lesta Studios in St. Petersburg Russia, *World of Warships* (PC) currently has over 44 million registered players – playing on five main servers across the globe. Over 500 dedicated staff members work on a four-week update cycle to bring new features, ships, and mechanics to the game – keeping game play fresh and inviting to new players. The game features over 400 ships, spread across 12 different in game nations. Ships are designed based on historical documents and actual blueprints from the first half of the 20th century, and it takes from two to six man-months on average to create each of these ships. There are over 20 ports to choose from, and 10 of them are recreated based on historical harbors and port towns.

There are four different ship classes: destroyers, cruisers, battleships, and aircraft carriers; with each class offering a different gameplay experience. Submarines have been in testing cycles since 2018, based on testing results and players' feedback then they have undergone significant changes that should allow them to launch as the fifth class in the near future. Ships are arranged in tiers between I and X, players must progress through ship classes and tiers to reach tier X. Ships of tier X represent the pinnacle of naval engineering from World War II and the early Cold War era. Each warship needs a naval commander to lead it into the battle. There are many commanders to choose from in World of Warships, including over 10 iconic historical figures. In World of Warships players can battle on more than 40 maps. There are seven different permanent or seasonal Battle Types to choose from: Co-op Battles, Random Battles, Ranked Battles, Clan Battles, Brawls, Scenarios and Training. From time-to-time additional Event battles are held. Additionally, within Battle Types there are four different Battle Modes available: Standard, Domination, Epicenter and Arms Race.

Tirpitz made her *World of Warships* PC debut in September 2015 as a Premium German tier VIII and was an instant fan favorite. Her good vertical armor and turtle-back provide excellent protection, fast speed, and a variety of armaments make her a formidable opponent. Like other German battleships, her main guns are less accurate than American or Japanese contemporaries, but it is her vast secondary battery which really shines—enemy ships will need to think twice before approaching her, and if they do, *Tirpitz* is also equipped with a quadruple torpedo launcher on each side just in case! Pick *Tirpitz* up in the premium shop and sail her into battle in *World of Warships* and *World of Warships: Legends* today!

Developed by the team behind *World of Warships* for PC, *World of Warships: Legends* is a completely new entry in Wargaming's flagship nautical franchise that takes full advantage of the power and capabilities of home consoles. *World of Warships: Legends* brings the online naval action loved by millions to home consoles for the very first time, alongside a host of content and features exclusive to the console experience. *World of Warships: Legends* is now available to download

Oberleutnant zur See in his "light" duty uniform—a dark double-breasted jacket without shoulder marks, and a summertime peaked cap. The duty uniform of the Kriegsmarine's officers differed in just a few details from the uniform of the Imperial German Navy's officers. Crowns disappeared or were replaced with stars, Third Reich insignia were introduced, and the stand-up collar gave way to a turn-down collar.

from the PlayStation® Store and Microsoft Store. Players can now wage wars across a variety of maps, in numerous warships and enjoy stunning oceanic vistas with glorious HDR support on PlayStation®4 and Xbox One X. Full 4K support is available on PlayStation®4 Pro and PlayStation®5, Xbox One X too! *Legends* also supports standard high-def on PlayStation®4 and Xbox One with more intriguing graphics on the horizon.

Wargaming proudly supports various charitable causes that members of the gaming and history community deeply care for. Supporting veterans and servicemembers: Operation Lifeboat (2020) raised $150,000 USD for Stack Up's mental health awareness helpline, Remembrance charity drive (2020) raised $45,000 USD for Help for Heroes, who supports UK veterans and service members, and Project Valor (2017) saw WoWS, WoT, and WoWP collectively raising $75,000 USD for a veteran housing program. Preserving historical ship museums: *World of Warships* partners with museums across the world to support the preservation of naval history and the education of the global community, with $50,000 USD raised for the restoration of USS *Batfish* (2019) and $400,000 USD raised for the restoration of USS *Texas* (2017). Finally, supporting the local community: a 24-hour charity livestream (2019) raised $43,000 USD for the Save the Children organization, and $78,000 USD for Team Rubicon and the victims of Hurricane Harvey in 2017.

Bismarck Günther Lütjens

Vizeadmiral Günther Lütjens (1889–1941) went down in history as the man who led the first, and only, voyage of battleship *Bismarck*, although he also took part in other significant military operations over the course of his career. Impermeable and a man of few words, but unreservedly devoted to his duty, Lütjens enjoyed an impeccable reputation among his superiors and unquestioned authority among his subordinates.

Tirpitz was still in the process of working up and crew training when *Bismarck* made her infamous maiden voyage, and despite requests for *Tirpitz* to join her brother—she was denied. The two siblings never sailed together in the Atlantic, and *Tirpitz* would be relegated to artic convoy raiding and hiding in Norwegian fjords for the rest of her career—earning her the nickname "The Lonely Queen of the North."

The United States Naval Institute (USNI) has been a proud partner of *World of Warships* and Wargaming since December of 2019. Wargaming has a made a commitment to naval history through various programs and events of over the past years. They produce excellent video content with their *Naval Legends* series on YouTube, and host events aboard museum ships where members of the gaming and naval history community can get together and experience the living-history in person. *World of Warships* and Wargaming are also great sponsors of HNSA (Historic Naval Ships Association). USNI thanks Wargaming and *World of Warships* for their continued support of the naval history community and participation in this *Naval History Special Edition*. Please see the back cover for a special offer for *World of Warships* PC and *World of Warships: Legends*.

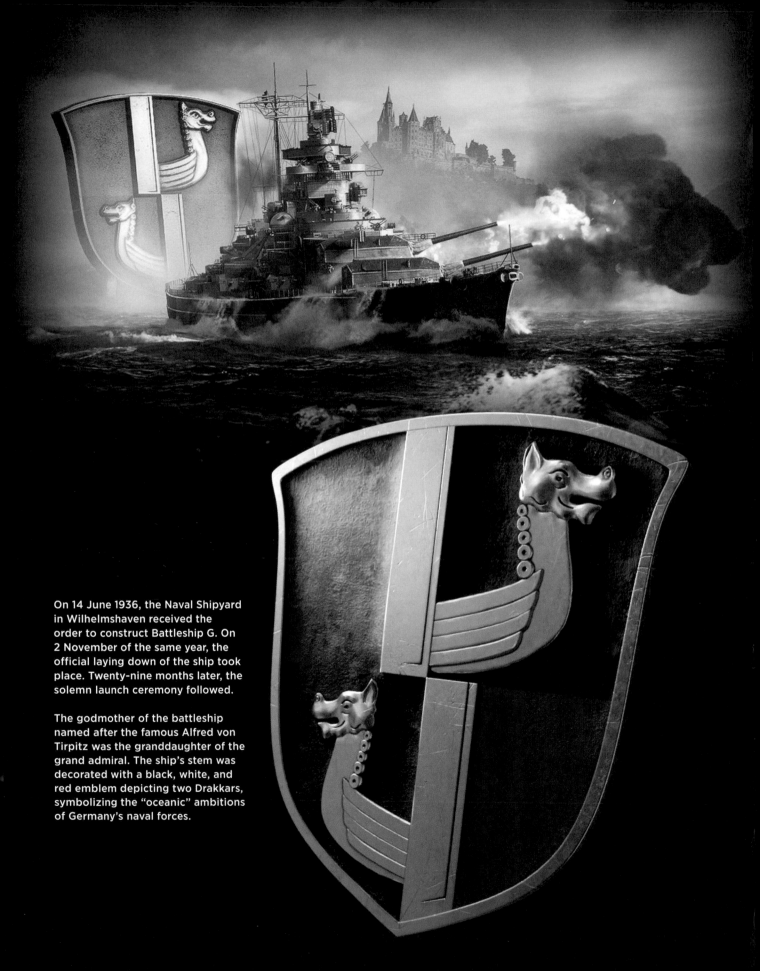

On 14 June 1936, the Naval Shipyard in Wilhelmshaven received the order to construct Battleship G. On 2 November of the same year, the official laying down of the ship took place. Twenty-nine months later, the solemn launch ceremony followed.

The godmother of the battleship named after the famous Alfred von Tirpitz was the granddaughter of the grand admiral. The ship's stem was decorated with a black, white, and red emblem depicting two Drakkars, symbolizing the "oceanic" ambitions of Germany's naval forces.

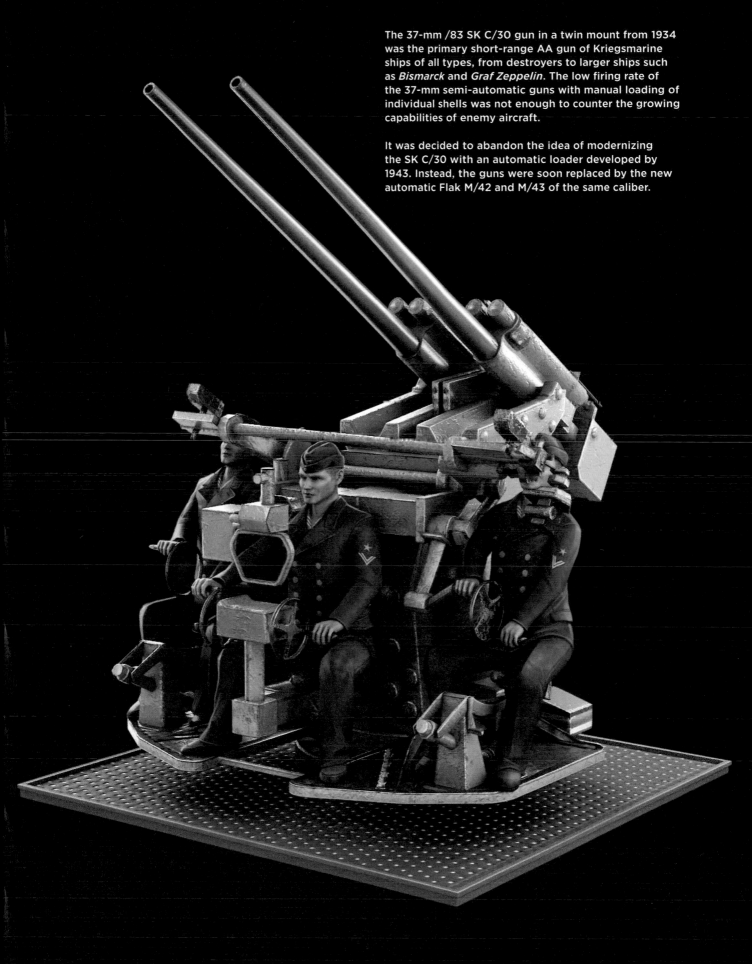

The 37-mm /83 SK C/30 gun in a twin mount from 1934 was the primary short-range AA gun of Kriegsmarine ships of all types, from destroyers to larger ships such as *Bismarck* and *Graf Zeppelin*. The low firing rate of the 37-mm semi-automatic guns with manual loading of individual shells was not enough to counter the growing capabilities of enemy aircraft.

It was decided to abandon the idea of modernizing the SK C/30 with an automatic loader developed by 1943. Instead, the guns were soon replaced by the new automatic Flak M/42 and M/43 of the same caliber.

Naval History Special Editions

8½ x 10¾ | Paperback | **$19.95**

Building upon the expertise of the authors and historians of the Naval Institute Press, the *Naval History* Special Editions are designed to offer studies of the key vessels, battles, and events of armed conflict. Using an image-heavy, magazine-style format, these Special Editions should appeal to scholars, enthusiasts, and general readers alike.

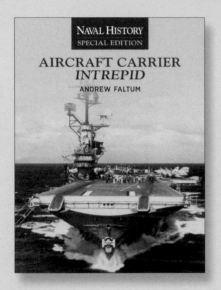

Aircraft Carrier *Intrepid*
BY ANDREW FALTUM
978-1-68247-740-3

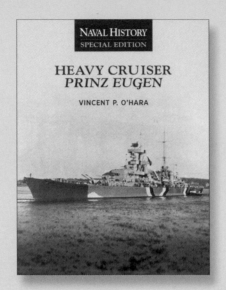

Heavy Cruiser *Prinz Eugen*
BY VINCENT P. O'HARA
978-1-59114-872-2

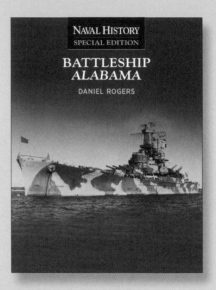

Battleship *Alabama*
BY DANIEL ROGERS
978-1-59114-698-8

Naval Institute Press publications you might enjoy:

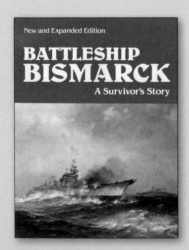

978-1-55750-436-4

Paperback | 🄴

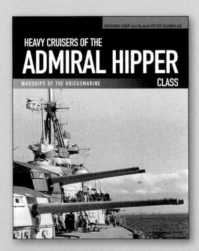

978-1-59114-168-6

Paperback | 🄴

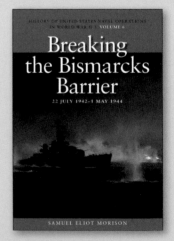

978-1-59114-552-3

Paperback